ACCELERATE

YOUR

WEALTH

IT'S YOUR MONEY, YOUR CHOICE!

DALE GILLHAM

First published in April 2018 by Stonehenge Publishing Pty Ltd
Reprinted April 2020

Cover design by Harrison Bouthoorn-Ashcroft and Zeno Kobica

The moral rights of the author have been asserted

National Library of Australia Prepublication Data Service:

Creator:	Gillham, Dale, 1962- author.
Title:	Accelerate Your Wealth: It's Your Money, Your Choice!
ISBN:	978-0-646-98534-3 (paperback)
	978-0-646-98595-4 (e-book)

A catalogue record for this book is available from the National Library of Australia

Disclaimer

The material in this publication is not intended to be taken or relied upon as specific investment or financial advice. The author and the publisher shall not be liable in respect of any claim arising out of any reliance on the information in this book. At the time of writing, all information, including prices and interest rates, is, as far as the author can ascertain, correct. Readers should always obtain independent or professional advice before acting on any information in this book.

What Others Are Saying

Accelerate Your Wealth explains how to go about trading like Dale Gillham is in the room talking to you. He argues that a low-risk, long term approach to trading the stock market is for the small investor, despite the many cynics who advise otherwise. *Accelerate Your Wealth* provides down to earth practical advice and tackles head on some of the most commonly held investment myths that hold you back from creating real wealth. More importantly, he provides detailed, tested trading principles to trade blue chip stocks to profit from the stock market. *Accelerate Your Wealth* is a great resource for those wanting to profit from trading over the short, medium or long term.

Tony Hunter, Former Head of Education, Australian Securities Exchange

Accelerate Your Wealth is an enlightening and educational read that sheds light on the keys to achieving financial freedom. Dale Gillham takes a simple, yet comprehensive approach to a rather complex subject. I highly recommend this book to traders and investors looking to hone their skills whilst seeking a life of financial independence.

Kritika Seksaria, Editor, Your Trading Edge *magazine*

Congratulations on another great book, Dale. You are committed to helping people beat the managed funds, and you are not afraid to tell it how it is—teaching people how not to lose money in good and bad times. Thank you for sharing your wisdom.

Jason McMillan, Graduate, Brisbane, QLD

Accelerate Your Wealth is a book I wish had read before I commenced my journey into share trading. It brilliantly and slowly guides you through the steps necessary to becoming a successful trader or investor—an easy to follow roadmap to safely and successfully trade financial markets. Dale has a unique ability in sharing his wealth of knowledge and I would recommend this book to anyone interested in learning the concepts to successful and profitable share trading.

Suzanne Burke, Trader, Hobart, TAS

Accelerate Your Wealth is a "vault of golden nuggets" for new or existing traders wanting to achieve greater success. Dale begins by unmasking the trading myths and misinformation before he clearly articulates the key disciplines critical to preserving your capital and building and managing a portfolio to maximise returns for growing wealth. Essential reading if you want to achieve longevity as a trader. Highly recommended!

Paul Henderson, Trader, Bangalow, NSW

A must read for every trader and investor: If you are starting out on your journey, it will give you a great solid base of where to start and, more importantly, how not to lose all your hard earned savings in the early years. If you are experienced, it will reinforce why you are trading and how it is that the simple strategies work— you don't need to overcomplicate your trading to be profitable.

Sharon Gleeson, Trader, Bendigo, VIC

I have known Dale for a few years now and one thing you notice about him is that he has a genuine passion for helping people take control of their own financial future, by imparting the knowledge and skills needed to trade successfully in the stock market. *Accelerate Your Wealth* does just that. It provides sound practical advice and an understanding of how to manage risk, by putting into place rules to protect your capital and the tools needed to enable an individual to start trading successfully in the stock market with a level of understanding and confidence. I highly recommend this book, not only to those starting out in the stock market but also to those who have been investing or trading for some time. It provides solid ground on which to build a profitable portfolio.

Barry Ward, Trader, Sydney, NSW

Wherever you are on your trading journey, this book has something for everyone. Written in a concise and easy-to-read conversational tone, it explains gently but firmly the fundamental key concepts, the logical objective approach and the tools you need to master in order to run a profitable share portfolio with confidence. There is profound wisdom within these seemingly simple concepts. Read this book and then read it again. Focus on its lessons and you will accelerate your wealth with ease.

Jane Pervan, Graduate, Hobart, TAS

Accelerate Your Wealth provides you with some simple, common sense strategies to become profitable in the stock market. Dale gives the reader a solid foundation to trading the stock market as he covers everything from portfolio construction, stock selection, money and risk management, psychology and more to get you started on the road to growing your wealth. A must read.

Sue-Ellen Kirby, Graduate, Melbourne VIC

If trading the stock market has ever crossed your mind or perhaps even overwhelmed you, *Accelerate Your Wealth* is truly the key to unlocking your potential to not only creating your own wealth but becoming responsible for your own destiny. Whatever your level of knowledge or competency, you will find much to stimulate your thinking about how to accelerate your wealth. Once again, Dale helps you think more clearly and less emotionally with the variety of data explored, and the ease of taking control of your own wealth—a truly mechanical and unemotional approach to a rewarding destiny.

Kerrie Taylor, Trader, Melbourne, VIC

Dale delivers, once more, a concise, simple and no nonsense approach to making money in the stock market. *Accelerate Your Wealth* is filled with practical, straightforward and common sense strategies to assist readers to truly create wealth. In his characteristic succinct writing style, Dale outlines some very simple, yet effective techniques that, if applied with discipline, have the potential to outperform those employed by the majority of fund managers. Most importantly, from my point of view, these techniques, when applied consistently over time, also help manage the emotions that inevitably get triggered when your hard earned cash is on the line. For me, one of the hardest lessons as a trader was overcoming the anxiety associated with losing money. *Accelerate Your Wealth* gives careful consideration to this aspect of trading and instructs readers to put risk management in sharp focus and most importantly, how. Perhaps after all his experience, he knows better than anyone, just how important it is to sleep well each night. For those wanting to take charge of their own wealth creation and do so safely with the benefit of timeless guidance and tried and true strategies for trading financial markets, I have no hesitation in recommending *Accelerate Your Wealth* to both beginners and seasoned traders alike.

Erica Bacon, Trader, Brisbane, QLD

Accelerate Your Wealth is for anyone who may be new to the market or who has been in the market for a while and wants to gain more of the right knowledge to succeed. I wish I had the opportunity to read this book thirteen years ago when I ventured into share trading, as I would have avoided so many mistakes. Thank you, Dale, for your dedication in writing *Accelerate Your Wealth* and helping so many people like me, understand the stock market and, gain confidence and knowledge. I know you have a passion to see people succeed and become financially independent and, that's why you give your all for this worthy course.

Jane Kamiti, Trader, Sydney, NSW

Accelerate Your Wealth is a worthy successor to Dale's first book "How to Beat the Managed Funds by 20%". This book should be valued and read by anyone wishing to participate in the Australian stock market. Dale's clear and succinct writing style gives the reader all the important tools and perspective to successfully trade the market in my view. It is refreshing to read a book which shows classical technical analysis techniques and how to apply them.

Warren Murnane, Trader, Burringbar, NSW

Accelerate Your Wealth is a "must read". It contains brilliantly written, easy to understand proven structured strategies, offering a reflection of Dale's profound experience and skill in the trading and investment industry. The content is unparalleled to anything I have read on trading or investing in the stock market. With detailed advice from researching stocks, to buying and selling, this is an asset for any person that wishes to trade or invest to obtain greater knowledge on how to fine tune their skills and be profitable in any type of market, with or without experience. Practicing the money management rules Dale has shared in *Accelerate Your Wealth* will not only increase your profits, but also assist with the emotional and psychological aspects so you become more profitable in your financial journey to accelerating your wealth.

Tracey Hutchinson, Trader, Adelaide, SA

Accelerate Your Wealth is easy to read, simple to understand and provides a practical "must read" guide to profiting from the stock market. It offers real life trading examples over challenging periods in the stock market that show, while not all trades will be winners, one of the most effective ways to make money in the market is to keep it simple and to always have a plan.

Ben Frost, Trader, Townsville, QLD

I have just finished reading *Accelerate Your Wealth* and I wasn't disappointed. I am impressed that Dale has been able to put so much knowledge into such a short story. The book is comprehensive, easy to read and understand, and so engaging with the psychology component encouraging one to take stock. If I had not completed the Diploma and Advanced Diploma I would certainly be planning on enrolling after reading this. Thank you for giving me the honour of commenting on the book.

Kate Gleave, Trader, Kuranda, QLD

Contents

"There is a great difference between playing to win and playing not to lose."

Daniel S. Dent

Foreword

Writing a foreword for a book on creating wealth is not something I ever expected to be asked to do, but in some ways I may be the perfect choice. I have long argued on 3AW that as a society, we fail our children by not empowering them with enough knowledge about money, how to manage it, and what to do with it. Put simply, one of the most important life skills is largely overlooked in the education system, and you can only presume the cost to society for its omission. I often wonder how I may have fared if I'd learned some sound basic skills related to money and investing before I made my way into the workforce. I have made plenty of mistakes!

I have been fortunate in my career, which has been largely due to a strong work ethic and being ready for opportunities when they've come along and as I head towards fifty years in the entertainment/media industry I'm still busy with radio, live shows, endorsements, and recording commitments. Having mentioned that, I have never had great skills financially like a Dale Gillham, and although I've nothing to complain about, it's easy to sometimes wonder what you could have achieved in a financial sense if you'd had the tools at hand and put them to good use.

Accelerate Your Wealth is full of great advice and will provide a wonderful tool for investors and traders alike. As Dale suggests, people should perhaps test his ideas in a small way to start with and grow from there.

Denis Walter, OAM
Broadcaster / Media Personality

Acknowledgements

Writing a book is always exciting and what I share with you in the pages that follow comes from over thirty-five years of meeting, learning from and being mentored by some amazing people.

In my life, I have been blessed by a small group of people who not only know who I can be and what I am capable of, but who, more importantly, expect more of me than I do of myself. This has made me a better person. These people have given me the strength, courage and support to explore and take on challenges on my road to success.

None of these are more important than my best friend and wife, Lea, whose absolute love, trust and faith in me has allowed me to achieve my goals and become who I am. There are not enough words to convey what she does or who she is. She is the life and driving force behind our business.

They say behind every good man stands a good woman and I have two—my wife and Janine Cox, who has been standing alongside us at the coalface of our business for over fifteen years. She is my loyal friend and sometimes sparring partner who pushes me to be a better person all of the time.

To those clients, who have put in the effort, placed their trust in our integrity, and given us the privilege of helping them to achieve their financial goals…

To our dedicated staff, who have committed whole-heartedly to ensuring our clients gain an education that is second to none…

To my friends and family, who have supported and encouraged me over the years to achieve my dreams and goals…

Last but not least, to our editor, Sara Litchfield…

This book is dedicated to you all. Thank you.

A Note to the Reader

"The only person you are destined to become is the person you decide to be."

Ralph Waldo Emerson

Over thirty-five years ago, when I started my career in the financial services industry, I was told by a wise friend that investing without knowledge was gambling. At the time, I tended to agree, but it wasn't until I started my own investment portfolio that I really understood the essence of this message. Many of my friends and colleagues were already investing in the stock market and, despite what seemed like good advice from friends and experts, they all seemed to achieve very mediocre returns. This intrigued me and what I came to discover was that if I wanted to control my own financial destiny, I had to invest time in gaining the knowledge and experience to invest safely and confidently.

Throughout the years, I have learnt many lessons, but the one that stands out the most is that you only get out of life what you put in. There is nobody more interested than you in providing for your future and ensuring you achieve financial independence. Yet, so many people are quick to hand over control of their financial future in the hope that other people will achieve better returns in the stock market than they could on their own. Given that so many others are interested in your money and it's not even theirs, doesn't it make sense to take some time to educate yourself so you can make confident financial decisions about your future?

The financial services industry is booming, but, increasingly, people are challenging the ability of fund managers to achieve adequate returns. And rightly so! Given that at least 80 per cent of fund managers underperform, you have to question why investors would want to continue paying ongoing management fees for so-called expertise in expectation of below-average returns. It's just not right.

Those disheartened by poor returns have let their feet do the talking by deserting fund managers and financial advisors alike. This is proliferating because of the ease with which we can now obtain information about how markets work, spawning an increasingly sophisticated generation of investors. However, the uncertainty of what action to take or whom to trust means many investors are taking chances and blindly investing in the stock market. This needn't be the case.

In my first book, *How to Beat the Managed Funds by 20%*, I introduced readers to some simple yet effective investment strategies in order to show you how you can earn much more than the average return you receive when investing in an institutional fund. The intention was to demonstrate how, if fund managers were returning 10 per cent, you could make 12 per cent. Given the simplicity of the strategies, it not only amazed many readers, but inspired thousands to take control and invest directly in the stock market to achieve very rewarding returns.

How rewarding, you ask? Would it surprise you to know that the average annual return I achieved trading the top twenty stocks on the Australian market from 31 January 1997 to 30 January 2007 was 52.09 per cent, which equates to an annual compounded return of 20.03 per cent? In comparison, fund managers averaged an annual compounded return of around 8.40 per cent over the same period.

While my initial book was focused on encouraging those new to the stock market to take the bull by the horns and invest directly using a low-risk approach, this book is directed at the more active investor or those who consider themselves to be traders. My intention is to debunk many of the common fallacies perpetuated in the stock market and to introduce you to a different perspective when it comes to how you can confidently and profitably trade the stock market—a perspective that will allow you to substantially increase the profits you take from the market on a consistent basis. Indeed, despite the stock market trading well below the all-time high that occurred in November 2007, I will show you how, by using some simple but powerful strategies, you could have more than doubled the value of your portfolio over the past ten years and significantly outperformed the returns achieved by the majority of fund managers. While the portfolio in this book is traded over the years preceding publication, it is important to understand that the strategies I outline are relevant in any market condition now and into the future. Although the examples are by necessity, specific—the guidance is timeless.

Unfortunately, many newcomers to the stock market and even the experienced often overcomplicate the process of taking profits from the market. I tend to attribute this to two things—firstly, the experts in the financial services industry who make investing for the small investor seem complex and mysterious and, secondly, the marketers who advertise that they have all the answers to gaining riches in the stock market, when all they really do is fill their own pockets by running expensive seminars and courses that fail to deliver on their claims. I hope that by sharing the information in this book, I will be able to convince you to put your uncertainties aside and take charge of your own financial destiny. Irrespective of whether you are a novice investor or a more experienced trader, you will gain the knowledge you need to consistently trade the stock market for profit.

As you read this book, you will come to discover:

- How you can take control of your financial destiny by eliminating the myths and misconceptions that hold you back from achieving your financial goals;

- How to stop losing and start making money by applying the three laws of successful wealth creation;

- The secrets to building a profitable portfolio, including the golden rules to success in the stock market and the strategies for selecting a winning portfolio;

- The strategies you can utilise to narrow down the selection of stocks to place in your portfolio;

- How to master direction so that you trade with the trend, and increase the profits you take from the market;

- The power of compounding and the effect this can have on your investments, so you achieve your financial goals much sooner;

- The strategies you need to utilise so that you cut your losses short and let your profits run;

- How to increase your probability of taking profits from the market;

- The strategies you can employ that will enable you to trade for a lifestyle; and

- The simple steps you need to take to achieve financial independence.

Most people I know just want to achieve a good, safe return on their investments. Here, we take a no-holes-barred approach to doing so. In this book you'll find no bright lights, no bells and whistles—just straightforward strategies that will enable you to achieve your financial goals. Some of what you read will require you to change your attitudes and, in some cases, your bad habits. But I guarantee that if you follow my strategies, you will be able to achieve better returns than the majority of professionals and pocket the fees you would otherwise pay to have someone else manage your money.

That said, before implementing any of the strategies I outline in the book, I recommend you test everything to ensure it works for you. Over the years, I have attended many workshops run by individuals whose strategies seemed to make sense with regard to how to create wealth in their chosen field—on the surface. However, on further inspection, I often found that what they espoused was either not possible, too hard to emulate or simply not true. So, I urge you, as you read through this book, to keep an open mind and then test everything I have written.

The ease with which we can now access information about the stock market means your journey towards financial independence is much easier than ever before. The age-old excuses of having no time or money will not cut it anymore. However, while many of you will read this book and acknowledge that the information is good, some of you will do nothing about it, or you'll make a promise to yourself that you will get around to it someday. From experience, I can confidently say that "someday" never comes.

I urge you, as you read these pages, to reflect on how you can use this information to take action today and get started on your journey to financial independence. You have nothing to lose and everything to gain.

Dale Gillham

Chapter 1

Taking Control of Your Financial Destiny

"The world is moving so fast these days that the man who says it can't be done is generally interrupted by someone doing it."

Harry Emerson Fosdick

A lot of people have realised that exposure to the stock market provides a long-term solution to building wealth. Indeed, with the ease of access to technology and information, there has been a proliferation of individuals worldwide who have taken the bull by the horns and directly invested in the stock market. However, this trend has sparked the rise of a host of entrepreneurs and marketing gurus, touting their fame and fortune, each claiming to have the "magic formula" that will ensure you make incredible profits. No doubt you have heard the clichés: "No knowledge, no experience and no time? No problem!" Really?

Certainly, those new to the stock market seem to be attracted by the hype and supposedly quick returns that can be gained by trading highly leveraged markets such as Forex. Unfortunately, many of the people who have been influenced by these slick sales people have failed to make anything. Indeed, many have been left confused and bewildered because they have either been bombarded with contradictory information or given poor advice.

Many individuals are also quick to hand over responsibility for their future to financial advisers and fund managers, in the hope of achieving better returns than they could on their own. Why is this? While it is true that some investors don't have the time or inclination to directly invest in the stock market, could it also be because the financial industry promotes to investors that they need these experts in order to justify their existence?

In my book, if you are looking for the best person to handle your investments without any conflict of interest, look no further than yourself. Let's face it, whom do you trust most? The question remains: Do you *want* to take care of your own investments? Only you can answer that, but if you are willing to spend at least some time educating yourself, you will be in a much better position to make informed decisions. With the right knowledge, you will be able to invest safely and confidently in the stock market.

My intention in this chapter is to shed some light on the common fallacies that hold many back from investing directly in the stock market, as well as clarify a number of misconceptions for those who may already be investing but achieving very mediocre returns. Indeed, the investment strategies outlined in this book will demonstrate that successfully investing in the stock market is much easier, safer and more prosperous than many would have you believe. Once introduced to some simple but very powerful strategies later in the book, your confidence will increase when you view the stock market, and you will be able to make a significant difference to your bottom line.

The statistics don't lie

Anyone who ventures down the road to trading the stock market will eventually come across the statistic that 90 per cent of individuals don't make money. This statistic deems that over time 80 per cent lose, 10 per cent break even and only 10 per cent make money consistently.

An interesting point about this statistic is that it is not based on geographical region, age, gender or intelligence. Everyone aspires to be in the 10 per cent who consistently make money, but few are willing to put in the time and effort to achieve it.

When I give a presentation, I ask those present if they want me to teach them what the 10 per cent of people who make money know or what the other 90 per cent know. Every time, they say the 10 per cent. To me, the answer to understanding the 10 per cent is simple—to be truly successful, you need to do what the majority of individuals who lose money don't do. This may seem like a simplistic view; after all, you don't know what you don't know. So, how does someone who is inexperienced and losing money or achieving very mediocre returns work out, from the overwhelming load of information out there, what they should be doing?

Before we consider this, let's take a look at two of the most common pitfalls that hinder many individuals from achieving their goals in the stock market.

Lack of knowledge

Throughout my career, I have been fortunate enough to be involved in helping thousands of people achieve their financial goals. However, a common theme, which became apparent in the early days of my career, is that most people don't know where to begin their journey towards achieving financial independence. Interestingly, in my experience, little has changed despite the enormity of information available on this subject.

The cold reality is that investing in the stock market is one of the few things you can do where you know from the outset you will lose money. The issue I find is that while many people agree with this statement on an intellectual level, the majority never believe it will happen to them.

The irony is that most people seek out quick fixes to achieving their financial goals with the mindset that short-term gratification will fulfil their long-term needs. This is often spurred on by the proliferation of seminars available. Whether the strategies presented actually work for you or not is usually of no concern once a sale is made. Indeed, from experience, I can say that all you really gain is a little bit of knowledge and very little understanding.

Think about it: If I spent a few days with you learning how to do your job, do you really believe I would gain the required knowledge or experience to be proficient? It is highly unlikely. Yet, many people are blinded by the instant gratification that the stock market offers, plunging head-first into the market using complex strategies in the hope of profiting from their efforts. Sadly, many have lost their capital, or a substantial portion of it, trying to implement these supposed wealth strategies. As a result of these poor experiences, many do nothing or seek out advice from a financial planner or broker, believing this is their only hope of achieving long-term wealth. But is it?

What I've learnt from over twenty years of investing in the stock market is this: Gaining knowledge is one thing; it's gaining the right knowledge and understanding that is critical to your long-term success in the stock market.

When it comes to trading the markets, there is a vast difference between knowledge and understanding.

While self-education requires both commitment and work, what I have discovered, and what I share with you throughout this book, is that you don't need to be a genius or a rocket scientist to achieve consistently profitable returns in the stock market. In fact, I think it helps not to be a rocket scientist.

If it is your desire to achieve similar results, you will need to have an open mind. Be prepared to accept that you may need to ignore prior learning or change your attitude. The journey will be worth it.

The psychology factor

While lack of knowledge is the main reason why many who attempt to trade the stock market fail, coming in a close second is the psychology factor. It is common for individual's to act on emotions rather than logic, particularly when their money is on the line. The emotions of fear and greed drive investors alike, and without the right knowledge these emotions are often amplified, which leads to costly mistakes.

This is evidenced by the fact we receive many calls from people with little or no knowledge wanting to learn how to trade highly leveraged markets such as Forex. When asked why, they often say it's because they don't have much money or time, which is the exact reason why they should not be trading these markets.

But this attraction to highly leveraged markets is perpetuated by the false belief they can get rich quick, which often stems from greed. People believe that because they only have $2,000 to invest, their return on investment in a leveraged product will result in more profits than if they invested directly in the stock. Therefore, in their mind, the desire for quick returns is worth the risk, although, in saying that, they rarely, if ever, think about what they could lose.

Sadly, while this is a romantic idea it is a fallacy. The market doesn't care how much you think you know or that you might only have a few thousand dollars, it just does what it does irrespective of whether you make money.

And herein lies the challenge: If you do not have much money, you tend to be more emotionally attached to it and, as such, cannot afford to lose it. Therefore, if the trade goes the wrong way even slightly, the fear of losing kicks in strongly, which often results in poor decisions and losses.

Individuals then end up taking a micro view of the market by watching their trades daily or even intra-day, or, worse, they make their decisions based on the short-term market volatility. This leads to an even bigger sin of over trading as individuals chase the market in an attempt to regain lost capital or profit.

Those new to the stock market further compound their mistakes by exiting profitable trades too early for fear of losing their profit.

Fear is the biggest enemy of those wanting to trade because it is a much stronger emotion than greed, and it stems not only from a lack of knowledge or confidence in the individual's trading plan, but also their inability to execute the plan successfully. Fear only kicks in once a trade is placed—what leads us to that point is greed or the desire for quick and easy returns.

"Knowledge overcomes the two enemies of prosperity... risk and fear."
Charles Givens

Myths and misconceptions

While lack of knowledge and/or your psychology will hinder your success in the stock market, what keeps many from achieving their goals are the myths and misconceptions communicated by many in the financial services and wealth creation industry. These are designed to keep you from achieving true financial independence. But why is this?

For the most part, the industry is profiting from the uneducated, lining their pockets instead of yours. The view that investing in the stock market is complicated and mysterious or best left to the so-called experts who supposedly know what they are doing is a fallacy perpetuated in part by those in the industry who stand to gain from your anxiety and ignorance.

So, how does someone work out what they should be doing? If you are tired of listening to the marketing gimmicks or achieving substandard returns on your investments, I suggest you sit up and take notice. What follows will debunk much of what you have previously been told about achieving long-term wealth.

Why buy and hold is not the answer

Probably the most perpetuated myth in the financial planning industry is that you should "buy and hold" for the long term. The reason why most of us hear these words, however, is that the industry cannot time the market. The funds are simply too large to manoeuvre with any speed. Consequently, the public is cautioned through advertising slogans about the perils of market timing. But accepting that time in the market is more important than timing the market is probably the greatest downfall of anyone wanting to beat the market average.

Those wanting you to buy into this myth claim that "market timers" sell when a market is low and so end up out of the market when the inevitable rally occurs. They assert that "market timers" run the risk of being out of the market at the trough of a decline when sentiment is at its most negative and potential returns are at their greatest. To substantiate this argument, they suggest that if you are out of the market on the twenty biggest days that the market is rising over a ten-year period, your return will fall substantially. However, the inverse of this argument is that if you are out of the market on the twenty biggest days that the market is falling, it stands to reason that your returns would surpass the market average over any ten-year period. After all, markets don't crash up; they crash down.

The perils of time in the market

No doubt you have all heard the industry's catchcry that you need to be patient and invest for the long term, usually ten years or more, to yield an adequate return. But, in reality, this results in the investor experiencing a rising market around half of the time to compensate for the years that the market is moving down or sideways. Let me explain.

If you look at the chart of the All Ordinaries Index, Figure 1.1, opposite, the run up from the low in November 1987, following the stock market crash, to December 2002 looks impressive. However, if you had adopted a buy and hold strategy during this fifteen-year period, your average annual compounded return would have been 5.57 per cent. The Australian market then experienced the largest bull-run (rising market) in history rising from March 2003 through to the high in November 2007. If we include this period then the compounded annual return over twenty years has only increased to 8.49 per cent, which is not that spectacular, particularly given the length of the investment.

Apart from the rising market from mid-1984 to the stock market crash in 1987, where the market rose for forty months, and the run up from March 2003 to November 2006, where the market rose for fifty-six months, most bull runs were no more than eighteen months to two years in length before the market turned down or moved sideways for roughly the same period. If you held a portfolio of shares from March 2003 through the long bull market and subsequent bust into the low in February 2009 as a result of the Global Financial Crisis (GFC), your compounded return would have been around 2.90 per cent plus dividends over this six-year period. And if we look at the ten years from 1 January 2007 through to 31 December 2016, your only profit would have been from the dividends you received as the market closed just 1 per cent higher than it opened during this period.

From 1991 to 1995, the market rose just over 50 per cent, although, during that time, the market also moved sideways and down for thirteen months between October 1991 and November 1992 and then again for twelve months between February 1994 and February 1995. Combined, this means the market actually moved down or sideways for twenty-five of the forty-nine months, or slightly over 50 per cent of the time.

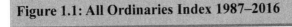

Figure 1.1: All Ordinaries Index 1987–2016

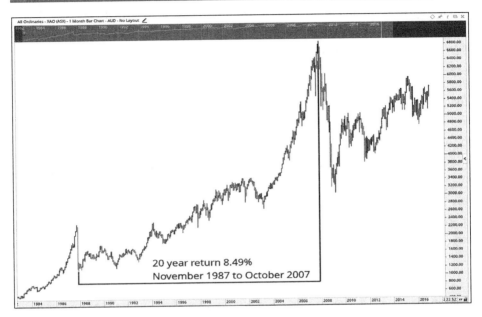

If we consider the 100 months from the low of November 1994 to the next major low in March 2003, the market closed higher for fifty-nine of those months. If we include the period from March 2003 through to February 2009, the statistic rises to around 65 per cent, although it falls back down to 59 per cent if we include the period March 2009 to the end of December 2016. And as you can see in the chart above, the All Ordinaries Index is yet to trade anywhere near the high that occurred in November 2007. Statistically, individuals borrow more money and tend to invest in the euphoria of a rising market, therefore, depending on when you invested leading up to the November 2007 high, anyone who applied a "buy and hold" strategy during this period would still not have recovered the losses they suffered during the GFC, despite the industry talking up returns over the past nine years.

In essence, using a "buy and hold" strategy will see gains during bullish periods in the stock market decimated when the bears take control in a bearish market, as we saw occur during the GFC and other previous major market declines. In contrast, with a little bit of knowledge, a more active approach will allow you to participate during the bullish run and sit on the sidelines when the market turns bearish.

The advantage of investing directly

For those in the know, timing the market is everything. Timing the market is about buying low and selling high, which is where the small investor has a huge advantage over fund managers. Getting it right will alleviate the problems associated with having your capital tied up for years in unproductive investments. Unlike fund managers, who must invest your capital when they receive it irrespective of whether the market is rising or falling, you have the flexibility to diversify the timing of your entry to ensure you only invest when the market is rising.

The flexibility to move smaller amounts of equity between stocks and to only be in the stock market when it is rising will result in creating a portfolio that outperforms institutional returns by a significant margin, which we will demonstrate later in this book. Selling stocks when the market is falling or moving sideways will enable you to compound your returns by selling shares at a higher price and buying more at a lower price. It will require you to be a little more proactive than an investor with a "buy and hold" strategy, but the outcome is worth it.

Later in this book I will introduce you to a simple strategy that will ensure you maximise your profits by timing your exit out of and entry into the stock market.

Don't dollar cost average

Another concept that has dominated the industry for decades is the notion of dollar cost averaging.

According to industry experts, dollar cost averaging can reduce the risk of investing in volatile markets and helps to avoid the "so called" pitfalls associated with "timing" your entry into market. The concept involves depositing a fixed dollar amount into an investment at regular intervals over a period of time, regardless of whether the market is moving up or down, so as to average the price at which you purchase the asset. Let's see how it works.

As shown in Table 1.1, opposite, let's say you invest $200 every three months into a unitised fund that initially had a unit price of $20. Over fifteen months, the market rises and then falls (causing the unit price to drop to its original value).

In this instance, while we invested $1,000 over fifteen months, we are now in a loss because we only have 43.32 units at $20, which equates to $866.60. Imagine if you invested in a fund that continued to trend down for years. I obviously don't need to say anymore!

The real emphasis with this strategy is the inability of the investor to "time" the market; consequently, they are encouraged to invest smaller amounts over long periods of time to take advantage of the fluctuations in the market. However, in my opinion, this strategy is flawed because not only has the investor lost the opportunity to invest their funds in assets that are rising in value, but they are taking higher risks investing in assets that are potentially falling in value with no guarantee of making a profit, which is ludicrous in anyone's book.

Table 1.1: Example of dollar cost averaging

Month	Contribution	Unit Price	Units Purchased
3	$200	$20	10
6	$200	$24	8.33
9	$200	$30	6.66
12	$200	$24	8.33
15	$200	$20	10
Total	**$1,000**		43.32

Diversify but not too much

We have all heard the saying "don't put all your eggs in one basket". There is good reason for this—quite simply, if you put all your money into one investment and that investment turns sour, you stand to lose all your money. Therefore, it makes sense to spread your money across different asset classes.

However, many in the investment industry also suggest that you should over-diversify within asset classes to minimise your risk further.

Unfortunately, in the stock market, this can not only dilute your investment returns but increase your overall risk because you require more time, knowledge and effort to manage your stocks. It will also condemn you to investing mediocrity.

In my experience, many investors hold far too many stocks (generally thirty or more) in their portfolio. Often, during my presentations, I tell people that, generally, one-third of their portfolio will be rising, one-third will be going sideways and one-third will be going down. Every time I mention this, most people nod their heads in agreement. After the seminar, many come up and tell me that this is exactly what is happening in their portfolio, like I'm some kind of genius.

Obviously, if you want to get better returns in the stock market, it makes sense to simply get rid of the stocks that are going sideways or down. After all, we only want to hold stocks that are rising in price, don't we? Assets that move sideways or fall in price have a negative effect on your overall ability to create wealth. If a stock is falling in price, it increases your risk and reduces your overall returns. Therefore, holding these types of assets should be minimised, if not eliminated.

To achieve better than the average returns, you have to concentrate on assets that are rising in value and increasing your wealth. Unfortunately, many advisers and brokers continue to reinforce the belief that diversification across a large number of stocks in different sectors will automatically increase returns. In my experience, however, the only people gaining from this advice are the ones giving it.

To achieve better than average returns, you have to concentrate on assets that are rising in value and increasing your wealth.

The reality of stock market diversification

While it is true that diversification reduces risk, a portfolio of shares that is over-diversified (for example, more than twelve stocks) is exposed almost exclusively to market risk, which cannot be eliminated by diversification. Let me explain.

An investor who chooses to invest in a particular market is exposed to the risks inherent in that market, such as the economic influences of inflation and interest rates that affect the market as a whole. Therefore, the market risk remains regardless of the degree of diversification of the portfolio. However, an investor must also contend with specific risk, which refers to the risks inherent in a company or particular events in a sector that influence specific securities. The total risk, therefore, is the sum of the market risk and the specific risk of the individual positions.

The specific risk is very high if an investor concentrates in only one security, but the more a portfolio is diversified, the less the specific risk. When diversifying a portfolio, it is important to know how much a specific stock serves to reduce the general risk. A stock from a different economic sector contributes more to risk reduction than a stock from the same sector because it is unlikely that all sectors will perform the same over time. For example, if one of the major banks is performing poorly, it is highly likely that all the banks will be performing poorly because they are subject to the same economic conditions. Obviously, the inverse of this argument also applies. This is why we are told that the greater the number of different stocks from various sectors held in a portfolio, the lower the specific risks incurred.

So, say the big four banks in Australia were all rising in price, for example; wouldn't you want to benefit from these returns? Not only would your portfolio be doing very well in terms of capital growth, but you would also be receiving income from dividends.

If all the stocks in your portfolio are in profit, how much risk do you think you are exposing yourself to? The answer is very little because, at any time, you can sell all or part of your portfolio and get the initial capital back after costs. In other words, the more the price of a stock increases in comparison to the price you paid to purchase it, the less risk you are taking with your capital.

Now, I can hear some of you saying, "But if I am holding all four banks, what happens if they all crash in price?" Realistically, the chance of all four banks falling heavily in price is extremely low. The reason for this is that institutional funds invest heavily in these types of stocks and it would take months for them to sell off their holdings in all four stocks.

Furthermore, stocks do not tend to crash at the top. If a stock is performing well, it is unlikely that investors will panic and sell (although, occasionally, you will get some big blue chip companies that do fall quickly). But, if you diversify into a concentrated portfolio of stocks, the likelihood of your entire portfolio crashing at the same time is extremely unlikely.

Over-diversifying a portfolio actually exposes you to market risk, which cannot be eliminated by diversification. Indeed, many people are beginning to question the conventional wisdom of over-diversification, preferring to invest in concentrated portfolios. The reason for this is, as Hoyle[1] phrases it: "You don't get twice the benefit from holding twenty stocks than you do from holding ten, and you certainly don't get ten times the benefit from holding 100 that you do from holding ten." Given this, it seems unrealistic to justify putting additional time, effort and analysis into finding other stocks when the diversification benefit is so small.

The truth of the matter is that to achieve maximum diversification and minimum risk, you only require between 5 and 12 stocks in a portfolio. In Chapter 3, I introduce you to my four golden rules for investing in the stock market. These will enable you to not only reduce risk, but also ensure your long-term success.

Cheap doesn't mean a bargain

Unfortunately, many newcomers to the stock market mistakenly believe that buying cheap is the best method for achieving higher returns. But this belief not only costs you money, it usually hinders your ability to generate profits because you are investing your faith in speculative stocks. In other words, you are speculating that a cheap stock will perform better than a solid blue chip stock.

I have lost count of the number of people who have told me they invested in a stock because it was cheap. So, just what do we mean by cheap? When someone states that a stock is too expensive, what they usually mean is that they cannot buy as many shares in comparison to a cheaper stock. The amount of shares you buy, however, is irrelevant to your potential profit. Let me explain.

When we buy shares, we do so with the intention of making a profit. If I have $1,000 to invest, I can purchase 2,000 shares at $0.50 or fifty shares at $20.00. If the shares rise by 10 per cent, do I make more money on the $1,000 invested in the $0.50 shares compared to the $20.00 shares? The result is exactly the same— although many would argue that the $0.50 stock only has to rise $0.05 to make a 10 per cent gain while the $20.00 stock has to rise by $2.00 to make the same gain.

While this is true, you also need to consider the chances of each stock making a 10 per cent profit. In my experience, the $20.00 stock has more potential to make a 10 per cent gain than the $0.50 stock, and it is far less likely to fall dramatically in price. Indeed, in a downturn, a quality blue chip stock will fall less than a speculative one and will generally recover more quickly. The $20.00 stock is also more likely to pay a good dividend, which means you not only get capital growth but income on your investment.

When a blue chip stock rises, it will normally increase at least 25 per cent in three to nine months, although it can move as much as 100 per cent or more in less than eighteen months. And while smaller stocks can rise faster in price achieving 50 to 100 per cent in weeks or even months, the reality of this actually occurring on the stock you own is less than 1 per cent. Consequently, you are speculating and taking higher risks, which can result in more losses and very average returns, not to mention the higher level of knowledge required to manage the risk when trading speculative stocks.

Furthermore, what seems slow is, in reality, much faster compared to the lost opportunity, loss of capital and, hence, loss of time you will expose yourself to when investing in speculative stocks.

In my experience, anyone buying a stock that is perceived to be cheap but still falling in value is gambling on a recovery at some stage. Unfortunately, buying cheap is fraught with danger and often a costly mistake.

When investors buy cheap stocks trying to get a "good buy", they usually end up saying goodbye to their money.

Indeed, when investors buy cheap stocks trying to get a "good buy", they usually end up saying goodbye to their money. Therefore, your aim should always be to buy quality stocks, not quantity, because this is where you will get the greatest gains.

The tortoise and the hare

The desire for quick returns on the stock market reminds me of a well-known children's tale from *Aesop's Fable*—the story of the tortoise and the hare. In this book, the hare is impatient, cocky and willing to take unnecessary risks to win the race. The tortoise, on the other hand, is happy to plod along at a steady and consistent pace. And we all know who wins, don't we? Unfortunately, I have met thousands of individuals who adopt the "hare" approach to trading. When I ask what returns they are getting on an annual basis, more than 98 per cent claim they get less than 10 per cent. So what is the moral of the story?

Slow and steady wins the race!

A slow but steady pace in regard to investing is much safer and far less stressful— both in terms of security (that is, the overall risk you take) and the potential financial reward.

Therefore, although contrary to popular belief, if you invest in top quality stocks and take a low-risk methodical approach to investing over the long term, nine times out of ten, you will achieve far higher returns than if you try to beat the market by picking the next boom stock or investing in penny dreadfuls. This philosophy is often ignored because, as humans, we believe we can beat the statistics. But the truth of the matter is that most investors actually end up becoming a statistic. Remember, it is not how much you make on any one investment that makes you wealthy; it is how much you do not lose over time.

In Chapter 4, I will introduce you to some simple but powerful strategies with which to filter the stocks to place in your portfolio and, in Chapter 6, I will show you how to manage a portfolio to achieve very rewarding returns.

Use leveraging wisely

The benefit of using leverage (borrowed capital) to invest is that it increases your ability to build an investment portfolio. It also allows you to take advantage of investment opportunities when you may not otherwise have the available funds to do so. More importantly, leveraging can increase the potential profits you receive from your investments, although, it can also magnify your losses. Therefore, you need to consider the risks of leveraging to determine if this form of investing is suitable for you.

Unfortunately, poor use of leveraging leads those who are unskilled to trade on emotion, chasing the market in the hope of attaining riches. Ignorance and overconfidence abound, particularly when trading highly leveraged markets, as people often mistakenly believe they can handle the fluctuating extremes that these markets present. The sad reality is that, for most, trading highly leveraged instruments is like giving the car keys to a ten-year old and telling them to go for a drive.

The truth of the matter is that unless you have proven to yourself that you can profitably trade stocks directly, you should never consider trading leveraged markets. If, once you have this experience, you are adamant that you want to trade leveraged markets, you should never invest all of your available capital. I will discuss why this is important later in the book.

Capital gains tax

Let's face it—most of us do not like paying tax. So much so that many investors often lose thousands of dollars because they are told by professionals to hold on to a stock that is falling in value rather than sell and pay capital gains tax. Indeed, it is widely publicised that we should minimise the capital gains tax impact of our investments. However, this costs you a lot of money and lost opportunity, which is why I consider it a myth.

If a stock turns and moves into a downtrend, falling over the medium to longer term, it will fall anywhere between three months and three years. And it is normal for stocks in a downtrend to fall a minimum of 30 per cent in price, which means it needs to rise 43 per cent just for you to break even on your investment again. In the meantime, you have not only lost money but also valuable time compounding the returns on your portfolio.

The amount of capital gains tax you pay will vary depending on how long you have held the asset. But, irrespective of this, doesn't it make sense to sell an investment you have made a profit on and pay tax rather than hold an asset that is falling in value and, so, lose profits? The amount of capital gains tax you will pay could be much less than the amount you lose. Let me explain.

Let's assume you invest $100,000 in ten different stocks with $10,000 invested in each stock. Six months into the investment, one of the stocks, after rising 12 per cent, turns and starts to fall in price. If you decide to exit the stock, you will be required to pay capital gains tax because the tax is triggered by the disposal of the asset. Given that you held the asset for less than twelve months, you will be required to pay tax on the total value of the gain, which in this case is $1,200 ($10,000 x 12%). If you pay 32.5 cents in the dollar tax, you will be required to hand over $390 to the tax office or up to $564 if you are in the top tax bracket. If, however, you decide to hold on to the stock and it falls 30 per cent in value, you will have lost $3,360 or $2,160 on your original investment.

Now, I can hear some of you saying, "What about brokerage and GST?" Even if you take all of these costs into consideration, you will still be far better off exiting from an asset that is falling in value. You will have retained all of your original capital investment plus the gain you made, which will enable you to invest in another stock that is rising, meaning your portfolio will compound more rapidly.

Trade well, not often

It seems that today, more than ever before, when I talk to people who want to learn how to trade, they tell me that their end goal is to "day trade" for a living. When I ask what day trading means to them, I usually get a myriad of responses based on ignorance because, all too often, individuals fall prey to the myth that trading more often means they will make far more money. In reality, the opposite rings true.

Unfortunately, many believe they need to replace one job with another and trade on a daily basis to achieve their financial goals in the stock market. This is often spurred on by professionals, such as brokers, who make money each time you trade. However, truth be told, all the brokers I have spoken with, have confirmed that the survival rate of traders who attempt to "day trade" is less than 20 per cent, although, I actually believe it's closer to 10 per cent.

The reason for this is that many people are taught to trade using daily charts. This is like having your face planted up against a brick wall; you are unable to see the bigger picture of what is actually unfolding on a stock or in the market. From experience, individuals who trade less, using weekly and monthly charts, make far more money and experience far less stress. Indeed, they have learnt how to trade in order to obtain a certain lifestyle as opposed to making trading their lifestyle.

I was recently talking to a trader who had been trading foreign exchange over the past three years and he communicated that he watched the markets all day from various computer screens. Now, you can imagine how stressful that would be. And given that he was enquiring about our education courses, you would have to assume that he was not doing that well. I actually said to him that, at a guess, if he added up all the hours in a week that he spent trading and then divided this into the returns he was making, he would get a better hourly rate working at McDonald's. He agreed. And the penny dropped.

Let me ask you, would you prefer to trade more and make less, or trade less and make more? Hmm…I know which I would prefer. The bottom line is that you will make far more money from strategies that enable you to trade well rather than often. I share such strategies with you throughout this book. In Chapter 4, I

You will make far more money from strategies that enable you to trade well rather than often.

show you a million dollar mistake that will change your mind about using daily charts to analyse the market.

Don't follow the herd

Would it surprise you to know that investors tend to sell winning stocks to buy losers, even though the winning investments they sell subsequently outperform the losers they continue to buy? The investor rationale for such action is driven by the fear of taking additional risks with stocks in which they have already made money. Unwitting investors believe that their winners, having already risen, are now more likely to fall. However, while this explains why investors sell winners, it does not clarify why they buy losers. For this we need to look at another factor known as herd mentality.

Many investors react to market conditions, stampeding up the mountain when the market is rising and sliding down just as fast when the market is falling. Unfortunately, this mentality is proliferated by the daily market reviews and sentiment expressed in the media. So what is it that drives us to follow the herd, particularly in the stock market?

Commonly, investors will follow the herd to avoid the possibility of feeling remorse in the event that their decisions prove to be incorrect. Herding also reduces the time required to properly analyse an investment decision on the basis of the belief that if everyone else is buying, someone else must have already done the required analysis. The reality is that many investors would rather purchase a stock that others are also buying in order to seek comfort in the knowledge that they are not alone in their decision making. It also enables investors to rationalise a stock that starts to go down; since everyone else thought so highly of it, it makes sense that they did too.

A recent study by two professors from Finland's University of Oulu, Conlin and Miettunen[2], purports that our investment choices are correlated to our personality type. The paper concluded that:

- Extravagant people favour large-cap growth stocks;
- Impulsive people favour small-cap growth stocks;
- Sentimental people favour small-cap value stocks; and
- Social people favour small-cap stocks (with a modest value tilt).

So, let's put this into context. Extravagant means having a propensity to spend or splurge; impulsive indicates a willingness to make decisions based on incomplete information; sentimental means having a tendency to be affected by emotional stimuli; and social means favouring joining groups and feeling attached to others.

The thing is, truth be told, none of these traits are good to have when it comes to trading the stock market.

Making money from stocks is all about deciding what the goal or risk profile of your portfolio is, and then matching the stocks you buy to that profile. You require an unemotional, disciplined process to follow that allows you to filter the stocks accordingly. Sadly, following the herd and being emotional just does not cut it when your goal is to make money. Your number one goal when trading the stock market is to minimise risk so as to protect your capital.

Protect your capital

A common misconception held by many who trade the stock market is that they only need to be armed with the knowledge of how to pick the best trades. This ignores the importance of knowing when to exit.

One of the most important aspects to successfully trading the stock market is to protect your capital. In the event that you are wrong and the share price moves against you, it is imperative that you apply a stop loss before entering a trade. A stop loss is simply a price point where you sell a stock to preserve capital if the trade turns against you.

Remember, successfully trading the stock market is about cutting your losses short and letting your profits run. So it's distressing to see many individuals taking on large losses and cutting profits. Recently, I was reading an interesting article on Forex traders that proves my point.

Rodriguez and Shea[3] stated that traders are generally right more than 50 per cent of the time; in fact, the ratio is around 59 per cent profitable trades versus 41 per cent losing trades. While, on the surface, this appears to be good news, when I delved deeper I discovered that the average loss on a trade was much higher than the profit and, in some cases, the losses were more than double the average profit.

Why does this occur? More often than not, individuals become emotionally entangled once a trade is triggered and, in the face of a loss, default to the "hold and pray" mentality in the hope of a recovery.

In reality, when it comes to trading and protecting your capital, a stop loss is your best course of action, as it will minimise your losses and it has the potential to maximise your profits. Indeed, the better you get at selling, the more money you will make.

In Chapter 8, I introduce you to a number of strategies that will enable you to protect your capital and, consequently, increase your portfolio returns.

To sum up

In my opinion, investing without the right knowledge is like jumping out of a plane without a parachute. It's just suicide. Unfortunately, the industry and many supposed "stock market gurus" continue to propagate the many myths and misconceptions about the market that keep you from achieving financial independence. In contrast, this book will help you cut through the marketing hype and equip you with the skills to invest directly in the stock market.

That said, to be successful at anything in life, you need to be prepared to devote some time to gaining the knowledge and skill to ensure you achieve your long-term goals. No one who has been consistently profitable has ever told me they got there through sheer luck or by taking shortcuts, and you shouldn't expect to either.

As the old saying goes, "wealth is the transfer of money from the uneducated to the educated", although, from experience, I believe it would be better put: Wealth is the transfer of money from the misinformed to the informed.

Wealth is the transfer of money from the misinformed to the informed.

If you want to be successful in the long term, I urge you to read on and become informed. What you will discover will change how you approach the stock market and allow you to take control of your financial destiny. Becoming part of the 10 per cent will require some effort on your part, but the rewards will be worth it.

Chapter 2

Stop Losing and Start Making Money

"A goal without a plan is just a wish."

Larry Elder

Financial independence is a goal many strive to achieve, yet only a few accomplish. The most common reason for this is lack of knowledge when it comes to how to create financial independence.

Many people believe that gaining a formal education will provide them with a job that will pay enough to enable them to obtain their desired lifestyle. Yet, the reality is that a large majority of people actually live from pay cheque to pay cheque, barely able to make ends meet. In an attempt to overcome this challenge, many work harder and for longer hours, believing the extra income will satisfy their needs. Sadly, most are already in a debt cycle and only wind up in more debt.

Why is this the case? The simple answer is that many people continue to live beyond their means. The desire to have whatever we want now and pay for it later usually means that we have to borrow money or use credit cards just to get by. Regrettably, many people become locked in a cycle that is ruled by fear. The fear of being in debt or going without money is what motivates us to work harder. But once we receive a pay cheque, the emotion of greed temporarily sets in as we think about all the wonderful things our money can buy.

It is the lack of knowledge about wealth creation that intensifies the emotions of fear and greed and prevents many from becoming financially independent.

We spent time in the previous chapter outlining why directly investing in the stock market is not as complex as others would have you believe. So, what exactly do you need to know to invest successfully? In this chapter, I will introduce you to the most important steps to developing your own wealth creation strategy. Although you may be tempted to bypass this information, believing you already know it, I recommend you take the time to read it; it will set the foundation for your future success.

Do you have what it takes?

We have all heard the saying: "If you fail to plan, you plan to fail." These words are so powerful, yet, so few seem to grasp the essence of what they really mean.

For years, I have listened to literally thousands of people share their desire to be financially free. For some, however, the overwhelming desire is just to get out of debt. Each of the personal stories I have listened to contains reasons as to why they are where they are. Although each story had its own personal circumstances, they were all intrinsically the same. You are today where you planned to be! No more, no less.

You are today where you planned to be! No more, no less.

Taking back control means taking responsibility for where you are now. If it is your desire to invest in the stock market, then you need to begin by determining your goals. We all have dreams and desires, but they remain just that until we make a commitment to take action. One of the tasks you undertake with a financial planner when determining what you want to achieve in the future is to document your goals and objectives. This helps provide the direction you need in order to achieve the financial outcomes you desire.

Your goals will be influenced by many things, including your age, your income, the size of your family and your current wealth. Some of the questions you need to ask yourself include:

- How long do I want to invest for?
- How much money do I require to achieve my goals?
- What returns do I expect to get?
- What level of risk will I feel comfortable with?

- How much investment capital am I willing to risk for the opportunity to make higher returns?

- Will the investment affect my social security entitlements?

- Do I require income or capital growth from my investments?

- Am I comfortable borrowing money to invest?

Once you have documented your goals, you need to make a commitment to take action—action to acquire the knowledge that will enable you to invest confidently and safely. Action coupled with knowledge results in prosperity. Quite simply, the more knowledge you have, the more confident you are going to feel about investing. With confidence comes a higher comfort level for taking risks. It also increases the likelihood that you will be able to discern between the right and wrong types of investment for you. In fact, Charles Givens got it right when he said: "Knowledge overcomes the two enemies of prosperity…risk and fear."

The road to achieving financial independence

As I have previously mentioned, one of the most successful strategies to creating wealth is to cut your losses short and let your profits run. While many would agree that this is a common sense approach to creating wealth, particularly when it comes to investing in the stock market, the reality is that many people still invest in assets that lose money rather than "financial assets" that create growth and income.

There are three laws of successful wealth creation that will enable you to stop losing and start making money. Many only give these principles a fleeting glance, believing that they already understand them and, therefore, do not need to give them the attention they deserve. But let me ask you—are you on your way to achieving financial independence? If your answer is no, then you need to pay attention. These principles provide the foundation for reducing your losses and increasing profits.

To know and do nothing is not to know at all.

The three laws of successful wealth creation are:

1. Spend less than you earn;
2. Invest your surplus wisely (at least 10 per cent of your income); and
3. Leave it alone so it can grow.

Of the many people that I have helped throughout my time in the investment industry, the majority do not get past the first rule of spending less than they earn. These people are unable to move on. Of those that do follow this rule and go on to invest their surplus cash, many fail to do their homework and, consequently, through lack of knowledge, do not invest wisely. Finally, even having invested wisely, there are those who are unable to leave their investments alone long enough to compound.

Let me reassure you that the fastest way to stop losing and start making money is to follow the rules above. After all, if you do nothing, that is exactly what happens—nothing. If nothing happens, you are, in fact, losing—as inflation steadily erodes the value of your money.

Spend less than you earn

Many people have asked me to show them how they can create wealth. In most cases, they expect that I will give them the "holy grail" of investing, the one thing that will make them millions. Instead, I ask them a question: "Do you have a budget?" You know—that great wealth creation vehicle that many suggest you should have to help you become financially independent. If you are like most people, you probably think that having a "budget" is difficult, that it is something that will restrict your spending, hamper your lifestyle and generally make you miserable. However, none of this is true; a budget is simply a financial plan that will help you to succeed and make a massive difference in your life.

A budget lists your income and expenses, and lays the foundation as to how you either invest or spend your money. Unfortunately, many see it as an angst-ridden exercise. They fail to put aside the necessary time to create one, preferring to do what is urgent rather than what is really important.

The thing is, without a budget, how do you know how much you are actually spending or, more importantly for your financial future, how much you can save? Only when spending habits are quantified do we know how much we can put aside. I have never met anyone who could not save at least 10 per cent of their income after completing a budget. Most people can save 20 to 30 per cent of their income and still maintain a good lifestyle.

Once you begin to budget, you realise how much money is wasted on uncontrolled spending. Budgeting is like your roadmap to financial independence—it provides you with a plan of attack that allows you to allocate your income appropriately so that you stop losing out.

There is an old saying that you can't buy new clothes until you clean out your wardrobe; you need to create space in your life so you can get more of what you want.

A budget allows you to create this space (cash flow) so that you have more freedom, more security and more wealth. Quite simply, it provides you with the flexibility necessary to plan for the future and, more importantly, take control of your life.

Invest your surplus wisely (at least 10 per cent of your income)

The second rule of creating wealth is to invest your money wisely. All too often, people do what is simple or easy rather than what is wise when it comes to investing. A wise investment, however, must have two components—it must give you capital growth (your assets appreciate in value) and it must give you income.

If the investment does not have both of these components, someone else is benefiting from the component you are not getting (which is, generally, the product providers you invest your money with). For example, if you invest in a bank term deposit, you will receive income but not capital growth. If your superannuation fund is in a unit trust, this investment has the potential to generate capital growth if it makes a positive return, but it does not provide you with an income until you retire. Investments that do not have both components are considered average investments from which you have to accept average returns.

The best method of acquiring both income and capital growth is to invest directly in property and stocks. Investing wisely in these types of assets is higher risk, but the reward is worthwhile, especially if you are willing to attain the knowledge and skill necessary to lower the risk and minimise your losses.

Given that you work hard to get your pay cheque, why wouldn't you invest the time in learning how to ensure your investments are profitable? If I work one hour to earn $30 and I invest that money in a stock hoping to win but, instead, I lose, that $30 can never be replaced—it is impossible for me to work that hour again. So why would I put my hard earned capital at stake unless I had a high probability of success?

To ensure you are successful, your investment strategy should satisfy the following criteria:

1. An exit strategy exists; and
2. You have a rationale for investing in a particular asset.

Let's examine these in more detail.

1. Exit strategy

One of the key criteria of astute investing is to consider when and how you will take your profits—in other words, you need to consider your exit strategy before you invest. Most investors never give this any consideration because when they invest, they expect the asset to rise. While the asset may indeed rise, the value of the asset is not realised until you sell. Consequently, this equates to unrealised profits, as the asset could fall in value. Therefore, you need to consider how and when you will exit if your investment turns sour or does not perform as expected.

Unfortunately, many investors mistakenly believe that if they have not sold a stock that is falling in value, they are not losing. But let me demonstrate why the opposite is true.

If I buy a blue chip stock that is rising in an uptrend, I know with high probability it will rise a minimum of 20 per cent in price over the next twelve months. Let's assume I invest in five stocks throughout the year. Four of the stocks rise in value (all by 20 per cent) and only one makes a loss (also by 20 per cent). Now, let's convert this into dollar terms. If I had invested $1,000 in every stock, I would have made $200 on each winning trade and lost $200 on the losing trade; therefore, I would have made $800 and lost $200, giving me a net profit of $600, or a 12 per cent return on my capital of $5,000.

Now, let's assume I decided to hold onto the stock that was falling in value, because I believed there was a chance it would turn around and start to rise. By the time it has decreased by 50 per cent in value, I realise that this is not going to happen. So, what is the effect of this on your portfolio? On the losing trade, you lose 50 per cent, or $500, meaning the unrealised net profit changes to only $300 ($800 - $500 = $300) or 6 per cent profit on your $5,000 capital. Allowing the losing trade to fall below 20 per cent halved the return on your portfolio from 12 per cent to 6 per cent.

The longer a stock continues to fall, the greater the effect on your overall profitability—which is why it is so important to cut your losses short and let your profits run. After all, you can always get back into the trade if the stock rises again in the future. In essence, allowing your losses to run into bigger losses turns a good investment strategy into an average one.

2. Rationale for investing in a particular asset

If you do not understand the consequences of your investment strategy, you are taking higher risks and there is a higher probability that you will lose. For example, many investors got caught up in the hype of the tech boom in the late 1990's, investing large sums of money in the hope of making a fortune.

Media hype and speculation fuelled the misconception in the marketplace that "blue chip" stocks were out-dated and that technology stocks or "dot com" stocks were the growth stocks of the future. This misleading information permeated the market, causing mass greed that resulted in stock prices skyrocketing to many times their true value. Many investors even forgot to consider the basic economic fundamentals of successful companies, ignoring that many of the "dot com" companies were yet to make a profit.

As a consequence, a lot of investors lost money and time that they could have spent creating a wise investment portfolio. And there is no doubt that this will happen again. Just look at the bubble being created by the hype and mania surrounding cryptocurrencies, which are a form of digital currency that appear out of thin air and then sky rocket in value to many times their worth.

Unless you understand the consequences of your investment decisions, it is better to invest your money in an average investment, like a bank term deposit. While your return may be lower, you are eliminating the risk associated with these higher risk investments.

Leave it alone so it can grow

The third rule of wealth creation is to leave your investments alone so they can grow. Einstein referred to this as the power of compounding or the eighth wonder of the world. When you invest wisely, your money will normally earn interest, dividends or capital gains. When you reinvest these earnings, it provides additional earnings because of the compounding effect. Consequently, this rule is the real key to wealth creation. Once you embark on your investment journey, you should leave your capital alone to allow it to grow.

Sadly, however, many investors prefer short-term gratification and dip into their investments to buy a car or go on a holiday or do something else unrelated to building wealth. If you do this, you need to be aware that it can potentially put you years behind when it comes to achieving your goals. This is because compounding produces only modest gains over the first few years. The real effect of compounding is only seen when your money is left for longer periods—then it begins to grow much faster.

Only when your investments are generating income and growth that is equal to or better than what you earn from working should you consider using your investments or income for lifestyle purposes.

A rule of thumb that I apply to all my investments is that if your return comes from investing, it should go back into your investments.

For example, if your tax return increases as a result of deductions from your investments, the increase in the return owed to you should be invested in other investments. Similarly, if you receive a capital gain from selling an investment, this should be reinvested in a new investment opportunity. Only when your investments are generating income and growth that is equal to or better than what you earn from working should you consider using your investments or income for lifestyle purposes.

To sum up

Taking back control means taking responsibility for where you are now. It also means being responsible for your future decisions and actions. Remember, there is an undeniable link between risk and knowledge. The more risk you take, the higher the level of knowledge required to manage the risk. But if you document your goals, and make a commitment to take action to gain the required knowledge and skill to invest safely and confidently, you will begin to see your goals come to fruition.

The foundation that will set you on your path to financial independence, so that you stop losing and start making money, is to spend less than you earn, invest your surplus wisely (at least 10 per cent), and to leave it alone so it can grow. These laws will work for you, if you work them.

Now that you have a better understanding of the laws of wealth creation, will you be one of those people who walk away saying, "Yeah, yeah, I already know all this?" If this is the case, I can only assume that you are already financially independent. If you are not, my challenge to you is to make a concerted effort to truly understand these laws and set yourself a goal to apply your understanding to your investments. Financial independence, like any other goal or desire, requires a plan or strategy. I have given you the foundation; the next move is up to you.

Chapter 3

Secrets to Building a Powerful Portfolio

"When a person with money meets with a person with experience, the person with experience ends up with the money and the person with the money ends up with the experience."

Harvey McKay

Over the past twenty years, at both commercial and social events, I have met literally thousands of people who either invest in or trade the stock market. Inevitably, the conversation always gets around to their portfolio and how they select stocks they want to buy and sell. A common theme among many of these people is a firmly held belief that all they need to be successful in the stock market is a "kick-ass" set of trading rules. Their focus is on achieving quick returns rather than setting the foundations required to build a solid portfolio. But this is like driving a car towards a cliff, only you don't know that the cliff exists, so you just keep driving...and we all know where that ends.

The unfortunate reality for many is that their investments are performing well under expectations. This can often be attributed to the individuals' lack of knowledge when it comes to how to select stocks and how to manage a portfolio.

In my experience, what investors need to be truly successful in the stock market is a practical framework that will allow them to select stocks for their portfolio that have a higher chance of ensuring that they are consistently profitable. Given this, my aim in this chapter is to provide you with a set of guidelines that will enable you to construct a portfolio that consistently performs, year in, year out.

The four golden rules to success in the stock market

Whenever I am presenting to an audience, I always ask how attendees select stocks. I must admit the answers always astound me. The most common responses include recommendations from newspapers, magazines and stockbrokers. Others include tips from friends, family and taxi drivers or the fact that they liked the name of the company or have used the company's products and services.

Let me say up front, this is not the way to select stocks if you want to consistently make profit; these methods are both inconsistent and ineffective. I have even discovered that most people spend more time deciding where to go on a holiday than they spend selecting stocks to buy.

Think about it this way. If you were to invest $500,000 in an investment property right now, how much time would you spend researching the type of area and property you want to invest in in order to be confident you will get a good return? Your answer, no doubt, is probably a lot of time. Now let's assume you want to invest $500,000 in one stock (although this is, in itself, inadvisable). How much time would you invest in researching not only how to invest in the stock market, but how to select the right stock so that you can invest your money safely and get a good return? Again, you would expect the answer to be a considerable amount of time.

The amount we invest, however, tends to change our perception of the risk we are taking and the research required to manage that risk. Usually, this is because it is much easier to swallow a $1,000 mistake than if you make a mistake with $500,000. But let me assure you, the process you take to invest $500,000 or $1,000 should be exactly the same; they both represent the same amount of risk.

What follows are the four golden rules I believe you need to consider when investing in the stock market so as to reduce your risk and ensure your long-term success.

Golden rule #1

Irrespective of the amount of money you have to invest or the instrument you are trading, you should always spend the same amount of time researching your options to ensure you are protecting your capital on each and every occasion.

Golden rule #2

When constructing a medium to long-term portfolio, you should always aim to have between 5 and 12 stocks in your portfolio (if you are an active trader, you may want to have closer to five). The idea is not to have lots of stocks with small amounts invested in each; instead, you only require a small number of the right stocks, with larger amounts invested in each. This actually lessens your risk and increases your returns because:

- Smaller portfolios are easier to manage and represent lower risk. The more stocks you have in your portfolio, the more work you need to do to manage your risk level.

- It is far easier to select a smaller number of stocks that are rising in price. The result is increased returns.

- You will have fewer transaction costs when buying and selling stocks simply because a smaller portfolio will have fewer transactions.

Golden rule #3

Never invest more than 20 per cent of your total capital in any one stock. If you invest in the stock market, you need to accept that some stocks will fall in value. However, this rule will help reduce your exposure to risk, while allowing you to achieve good returns simply because you are minimising the amount of capital you could lose at any one time.

For example, if you invested $100,000 in five different stocks, you would be investing $20,000 in each stock, or 20 per cent of your total capital. If, at the end of your first year, one of the stocks has dropped by 50 per cent, you will have lost $10,000 of your initial capital. But if the other four stocks have risen in value by 10 per cent, then you will have made $8,000. Therefore, your total loss would be $2,000, or only 2 per cent of your initial capital. In effect, you will have minimised your exposure to risk by spreading your capital across a number of stocks.

Golden rule #4

You should only ever invest 10 per cent of your available capital in trading short-term highly leveraged markets and allocate the remaining 90 per cent to trading a medium to long-term portfolio. This is a very solid money management rule that allows you to take a low risk approach with your money while still achieving good returns on your capital.

The goal with this rule is to have the 10 per cent allocated to trading short-term highly leveraged markets achieve equal or better returns when compared to the 90 per cent. Let me explain.

Let's say you have $150,000 to invest. You would place $135,000 in a medium to long-term portfolio and allocate the remaining $15,000 to short-term trading. Leveraging or trading on margin at 10:1, for example, you would have $150,000 to generate cash flow in your short-term trading account.

Now let's assume you need to make $50,000 in income per annum. If you averaged 11 per cent return on your medium to long-term portfolio of $135,000, including dividends, you would receive around $15,000, which means you only need to make approximatey $35,000 from your short-term portfolio.

In my experience, when trading leveraged markets, your watch list should consist of no more than ten stocks (or indices/markets) that you know inside out and you should hold no more than four leveraged positions at any one time so as to minimise your risk. Therefore, you would place no more than $30,000 (20 per cent of the $150,000 in your short-term trading account) in each trade. That way, you have the remaining cash accessible in the event of a margin call, which is the requirement for a debt to be reduced, or extra security to be provided, if the leveraged asset loses value.

Therefore, the $15,000 allocated to your short-term portfolio, traded on a margin of 10:1, only needs to rise around 2.44 per cent in a month to generate approximately $2,925 on your capital or the additional $35,000 in income per annum. This is not only very achievable but, more importantly, very repeatable when you have gained the required knowledge and skill.

Acquire the knowledge.
Create the wealth!®

Choosing a medium to long-term stock portfolio

If you have ever visited a financial adviser, you will know that they usually select a fund based on your investment goals and the risk you are willing to take. Referring back to the questions on your investment goals in Chapter 2, you may want to take some time now to document three financial goals you would like to achieve in the next five years.

1. _____

2. _____

3. _____

The answers you provide will assist you in selecting a portfolio of stocks that is suitable for you.

To assist you in the process, I have provided in Table 3.1, below, four different types of portfolios based on the level of risk involved. By no means are these the only portfolios you could construct, but they do provide an indication of the volatility associated with each investment.

Table 3.1: Portfolio selection and risk

Portfolio type	Description/risk tolerance
Superannuation	<ul><li>*Goal:* long-term growth of 10 years plus</li><li>*Features:*</li><li>low risk</li><li>return of 10 to 15 per cent including dividends</li><li>need stable income and steady growth in capital</li><li>will not accept fall in capital value</li></ul>
Blue chip	<ul><li>*Goal:* medium to long-term growth of five years plus</li><li>*Features:*</li><li>low risk</li><li>return of 10 to 20 per cent including dividends</li><li>accept some small fluctuations in income and capital</li><li>need little or no income stream</li></ul>
Growth	<ul><li>*Goal:* medium-term growth of one to five years</li><li>*Features:*</li><li>medium risk</li><li>medium return of 15 per cent plus dividends</li><li>accept fluctuations in income and capital to gain capital growth over the medium term</li><li>need little or no income stream and no need to access capital in the medium term</li></ul>
Mid-cap	<ul><li>*Goal:* medium-term growth of one to five years</li><li>*Features:*</li><li>medium to high risk</li><li>high return of 20 per cent plus dividends</li><li>no need for ongoing income or access to capital</li><li>accept wider fluctuations in income and capital to gain growth over the medium term</li></ul>

Regardless of whether you are looking for growth or income, you will need to select good quality stocks for your portfolio.

Identifying the right stocks for a medium to long-term portfolio

Identifying the right stocks to place in a medium to long-term portfolio can seem like a daunting task, particularly when you are faced with hundreds if not upwards of thousands of stocks to choose from. Indeed, all too often, people feel like the job is too big and that it will take up too much of their time. But this needn't be the case.

Step 1: Identify the goal of your portfolio

When selecting stocks, you should always keep in mind the goal of your portfolio. Obviously, the stocks you select for a growth portfolio will be different to the stocks you select for a mid-cap portfolio. On many occasions, I have seen portfolios constructed with the wrong stocks—it wasn't that the stocks were bad; they were just not suited to the goal of the portfolio. For example, many of the superannuation portfolios I have seen included resource stocks, however, many of these types of stocks do not belong in a superannuation portfolio simply because they are very volatile, subject to huge swings in price and, in some cases, pay almost no dividend.

In a superannuation portfolio, you are looking for long-term, steady-growth stocks that, over a period of time, reach higher prices and pay high dividends. Because of the tax advantages of a superannuation fund, the dividends should preferably be fully or partly franked (meaning some or all of the tax has already been paid on the dividends). If you were constructing an active portfolio for growth over a shorter period of time, however, resource stocks would be more suitable.

Step 2: Develop a watch list of stocks to suit the goal of your portfolio

A good place to start constructing a list of possible stocks is to identify the top stocks listed on the market by capitalisation. Market capitalisation is used to determine the dollar value of a company and is calculated by taking the number of shares a company has on issue and multiplying it by the share price. The stocks are then ranked from the largest company down to the smallest.

As discussed above, the goal of your portfolio will determine the amount of risk associated with it and, therefore, the amount of research you will need to undertake to select the most appropriate stocks.

Superannuation portfolio

Because you are seeking growth stocks that, over a period of time, reach higher prices and pay high dividends, I recommend you construct your portfolio using the top twenty stocks on the Australian Securities Exchange (ASX). If you also wanted to consider some stocks out to the top fifty, you would focus your attention on the S&P/ASX 50 Index.

This type of portfolio is easy to manage and requires very little of your time once established. Therefore, it is more suited to investors who have at least one hour a month to manage their portfolio.

Blue chip portfolio

This type of portfolio is best suited to people with a low tolerance to risk who are seeking a balanced approach between growth and income. Given this, a blue chip portfolio is mainly constructed (roughly 80 per cent of your portfolio) from the top fifty companies on the ASX, with one or two stocks selected from the top 50 to 100. This type of portfolio is suited to investors who have up to two hours a month to manage their portfolio once it is established.

Growth portfolio

This portfolio is suited to those people who are more risk tolerant and willing to spend more time getting a better return on their investments. The portfolio would be constructed using a mixture of the top 100 stocks on the ASX. Stocks from the top fifty would make up 60 per cent of the portfolio and 40 per cent would be selected from the top 51 to 100. This would give you stability from stocks in the top fifty combined with the growth potential of stocks in the top 51 to 100. This type of portfolio is more suited to those who have at least one hour a week to manage their portfolio.

Mid-Cap portfolio

This type of portfolio needs to be actively managed and is, therefore, more suited to those who have a few hours a week to allocate to managing their portfolio once it is established. A mid-cap portfolio is generally constructed from the top 51 to 150 stocks on the ASX. As such, it is higher risk than the other portfolios because the stocks are subject to more volatility.

You may want to consider holding stocks outside the top 150, although I recommend you never hold more than 10 per cent of these stocks in your portfolio at any one time. You should again weight your portfolio towards the safer stocks—60 per cent of the portfolio would come from stocks listed in the top 51 to 100 and 40 per cent from the top 100 to 150. Remember, the more you stray outside of the top 100 stocks by market capitalisation, the more volatility you will experience.

When you have a list of stocks from which to draw from, you will find two things happen:

- You will spend less time researching what stocks to buy as you will tend to ignore any stock that is not on your list. Many people spend more time researching stocks than they need to because they don't take a targeted approach.

- You will also be more profitable because you will spend more time getting to know the stocks that are relevant to your portfolio, which will enable you to pick the best stocks more easily.

Why you should only select the top stocks

The list of stocks you select for your portfolio will depend on the time you have available, your resources and the goal of your portfolio. That said, I recommend you don't stray too far outside the top 150 stocks by market capitalisation on any market for the following reasons:

- The top stocks are highly liquid—in other words, there is a lot of buying and selling taking place in these stocks every day, which means even in the event of a dramatic stock market crash, you will still be able to sell these companies quickly and easily;

- The top stocks are generally profitable businesses with some of the best managers, providing stability in the growth of the company and the stock price;

- The top stocks are purchased heavily by the institutions, therefore, they are less likely to be affected by mass panic buying and selling;

- Reliable information about these stocks is much easier to obtain;

- The chances of any one of these companies going broke is very small;

- Over a ten-year period, the majority of these stocks will produce very good returns from both capital gain and income from dividends.

Venturing outside the top stocks will not only increase your risk level but the knowledge required to successfully manage the risk.

Identifying the right stocks for a short-term portfolio

The desire to trade short term, for most people, is a result of the mistaken belief that they will make far more money from this type of trading than any other method. It also comes from the fallacy that by trading short term, they will become wealthier much quicker, particularly if they are leveraging their position. But this is simply not true, as most of the people who attempt this method of trading soon discover.

Of course, obtaining wealth quickly through short-term trading can happen. However, in my experience most of the people who have achieved this feat have done it by being extremely lucky rather than a skilled trader. Their greed and/or ignorance regarding what they were trading and how they traded meant they took higher risks in order to achieve exceptional returns, often during volatile times in the market. Sadly, most of these people believed they could continue trading the same way when the market normalised; the majority lost most, if not all, of what they had made.

If it is your desire to trade short term (and/or to use leveraging to accelerate your returns), you need to have developed a high level of knowledge and skill, as you are looking to take advantage of the swings in price that unfold over the short term. It is also important to remember that if you choose to use leveraging, just as it can accelerate your returns, it can also accelerate your losses. In my book, short-term trading (particularly if you apply leveraging) should only ever be used to complement your medium to long-term portfolio—it should not be the catalyst for building your long-term wealth.

Short-term trading should only ever be used to complement your medium to long-term portfolio—it should not be the catalyst for building your long-term wealth.

When constructing a short-term portfolio, the stocks you choose will depend on the level of risk you are willing to take. If you are more risk averse, you may want to consider stocks out to the top fifty by market capitalisation, however, if you have a higher risk tolerance, you may want to consider stocks in the top 50 to 150 by market capitalisation. The latter are more volatile in nature and can move anywhere from 5 to 10 per cent or more in a week.

The key to short-term trading, besides your entry and exit rules, is the liquidity of the stock you are trading, as you need to be able to enter and exit freely. Therefore, my rule of thumb is only to trade stocks with an average volume of $5,000,000 or more each day.

Remember, you should only allocate 10 per cent of your total capital to short-term trading with the goal of this portfolio to achieve returns equal to or better than your medium to long-term portfolio. And never hold more than four leveraged positions at any one time.

In reality, trading short term is something that requires both patience and persistence when it comes to watching the market and managing your trades. Therefore, unless you have proven to yourself that you can trade profitability over the medium to long term, I would strongly encourage you to build up your experience before attempting this strategy.

In the next chapter, I discuss how you can narrow down the stocks on your watch list to select those most appropriate for your portfolio. In Chapter 6, I show you how to manage your portfolio to achieve very rewarding returns.

How to construct a portfolio with different amounts of capital

Obviously, the amount of capital you have to invest will determine how you initially construct your portfolio.

Small investors

One of the most common questions I get asked is: "How much do I need to start investing in the stock market?" You can begin investing with as little as $1,000, although you will want to develop a savings strategy so that you can build up your portfolio until you hold at least five stocks. Because of transaction costs, I always recommend that the minimum amount you should allocate to a particular stock is $1,000.

Obviously, if you have less than $5,000 to invest, you will be breaking Golden Rule #3 until your portfolio grows large enough to ensure you only ever invest 20 per cent of your total portfolio in any one stock. But it's okay to break this rule in the short term; for many, it is the only way they can get started in the stock market.

Once you hold a minimum of five stocks, you can begin to increase the amount of shares you hold in each company. If you sell a stock, reinvest the capital from the sale into another stock, as well as any savings you may have accumulated, to increase the amount you are purchasing. Gradually your position size (the amount of cash you initially invest in any one stock) will increase, rather than the amount of stocks you own, which will ensure you are able to manage your risk.

If you have less than $5,000 to invest, it is not recommended that you consider leveraging as part of your overall portfolio strategy until you build up your capital to around $20,000.

Small to medium investors

If you have between $5,000 and $20,000 to invest, you may still need to break Golden Rule #3, particularly if you have less than $10,000, as you want larger parcels of your capital invested in stocks, so that you minimise your risk. Therefore, if you have less than $10,000, I recommend you split your capital into parcels of 25 per cent so you hold four different stocks.

If you have $10,000 to $20,000 to invest, you would comfortably invest no more than 20 per cent of your total capital in each stock. In other words, you would simply buy five different stocks to hold in your portfolio.

If you want to incorporate leveraging into your portfolio, I would only recommend this if you have $20,000 or more to invest. In this instance, you would allocate $18,000 to your medium to long-term portfolio and $2,000 to your short-term trading account, which would provide you with capital of $20,000 at 10:1 trading on margin.

That said, another form of leveraging, also called margin lending, allows investors to use their existing stocks to increase their investment portfolio. Generally, banks or margin lenders will loan up to 70 per cent of the total value of the portfolio. Therefore, if you have $30,000 in securities, you can leverage up to $100,000— the lender will finance you an additional $70,000 using a margin loan, so your total exposure in the stock market is $100,000. The total portfolio then acts as security on the loan. The upside of this form of leveraging is that the loan interest is tax deductible because you are using it for investment purposes.

To minimise your risk when using margin lending, it is advisable that you avoid using all of the available funds that the lender provides. Allow yourself a safety margin in case something does go wrong. For example, if you have access to $70,000, you may only want to consider using 70 per cent, or $50,000, of the available funds so that you only have $80,000 exposed to the market and retain $20,000 for any potential margin calls.

Larger investors

If you are a large investor with capital holdings over $20,000, you may want to purchase more than five stocks. This way, the percentage of your total capital that you invest in each stock will drop below 20 per cent. For example, if you have $100,000 to invest, you may want to purchase ten stocks, with each stock representing 10 per cent of your total portfolio. On the other hand, if you have a million to invest, you may want to invest $100,000 in each stock, which would still represent only 10 per cent of your total portfolio in any one stock.

Although I recommend you should never invest more than 20 per cent of your total portfolio in any one stock, obviously your portfolio will grow as the stocks rise in value. Over time, this growth will change the percentage each stock represents in your portfolio, as one or more rise in price. This is perfectly okay, as Golden Rule #3 only relates to the amount of capital you should invest when initially purchasing a stock. Remember—the purpose of this money management rule is to protect your total capital should a newly entered position turn bad.

For example, if your initial capital was $100,000, you may have invested $20,000 in five different stocks. If after twelve months, your portfolio has grown to $120,000, and you decide to sell a stock to purchase another, you would never reinvest more than $24,000 in any one stock. This is because $24,000 represents 20 per cent of your total capital of $120,000.

Those with larger portfolios are better placed to incorporate leveraging as part of their overall investment strategy, however, as I have stressed many times before, you need to ensure you are consistently profitable in the stock market over the medium to long term before you consider this approach.

To sum up

Let me say, from experience, if you follow the golden rules and strategies outlined in this chapter, you will reduce your risk and achieve greater returns than most in the stock market. Remember,

- Always take the same amount of time researching your options to ensure you are protecting your capital on each and every occasion.

- Always aim to have between 5 and 12 stocks in your portfolio.

- Never invest more than 20 per cent of your total capital in any one stock.

- Only ever invest 10 per cent of your available capital in trading short-term highly leveraged markets and allocate the remaining 90 per cent to trading a medium to long-term portfolio.

To ensure you apply a targeted approach when selecting the right stocks to place in your portfolio, you first need to identify the goal of your portfolio—in other words, are you seeking growth, or growth and income? Once you have done this, you then need to develop a watch list of stocks to suit the goal of your portfolio. You also need to consider the amount of capital you have to invest, as this will determine how you initially construct your portfolio.

Last, but not least, it is important, if you want to achieve better than average returns, to focus your attention on assets that are rising in value and increasing your wealth.

Now that you understand the golden rules to building a powerful portfolio, let's look at how you would construct a profitable portfolio.

Chapter 4

Constructing a Profitable Portfolio

"I can't change the direction of the wind, but I can adjust my sails to always reach my destination."

Jimmy Dean

Ask anyone who trades the stock market if they know how to buy a stock and, chances are, 100 per cent will say yes. Ask those same people if they know the right time to sell a stock and 90 per cent will say either no or that they get it wrong most of the time.

While knowing when to exit should be part of everyone's risk management strategy, the challenge with exiting a stock occurs because, fundamentally, very few really understand how to determine the direction of a stock or market. In fact, this lack of knowledge is so prevalent, it is like a black plague leaving wannabe investors and traders dead in its wake. As such, I believe the number one skill all individuals should possess, if they want long-term success in the stock market, is the ability to accurately identify direction.

Yes, direction...

No doubt, some of you will be thinking, "Is this guy for real? Of course I know how to determine direction!" But do you really? How often do you get stopped out of trades or have trouble working out the right entry or exit to trade? How often do you experience lots of little profits interspersed with big losses? Believe it or not, these are all symptoms of not really understanding the direction of the market as well as you could.

If you can correctly ascertain the direction of the longer-term trend, however, either bull or bear, you can pinpoint, with great certainty, the right time to buy and sell, which means you will be far more profitable. Obviously, the higher the return you desire, the more knowledge, experience and time you will need to devote to your investments.

This doesn't mean you need to look at the market on a daily basis—rather, it simply means you will need to commit some time to monitoring your stocks and managing your portfolio. Of course, the challenge is to develop a system that is repeatable, so that profitable returns are consistently generated.

Passive versus active

Before moving on to discuss the methods by which you can narrow down the selection of stocks to place in your portfolio and how to correctly analyse direction, let's consider the passive versus active debate when it comes to investing directly in the stock market.

Passive investor

The passive investor is someone who has little or no time in which to select and manage stocks in their portfolio. They want, however, to achieve good returns over the medium to long term.

If this is you, I recommend you stick to the top twenty stocks by market capitalisation and select between eight and twelve stocks based on the rules we outline later in this chapter. While it is not advisable to embrace a "set and forget" mentality, they are the top stocks on the market for good reason and, therefore, more forgiving. However, if you decide this is your only option, you must accept the potential risk you are taking is higher, meaning the rewards will be lower than if you actively managed your portfolio on a regular basis.

As your capital grows, you may decide to take a more active approach. From experience, I have found that once the passive investor begins to make money, they miraculously find more time to devote to managing their investments.

Active investor

An active investor, as the name suggests, is more proactive in selecting stocks and managing their portfolio, dedicating a few hours a month. Due to time constraints, the active investor's knowledge of the stock market is generally limited, although they do recognise that taking an active approach to managing their portfolio has the potential to optimise their returns. Typically, an active investor turns over, on average, 20 to 30 per cent of the stocks within their portfolio in a year, although this will depend on market conditions.

Given that the active investor is constrained by time, I would, once again, recommend developing a portfolio of between eight and twelve stocks from the top twenty by market capitalisation, although, depending on your level of knowledge, you may want to consider stocks out to the top fifty. As your circumstances change and you have more time, you may want to widen your horizons to include a few more stocks from the top 50 to 150, although this will depend on the type of portfolio you select.

If you are new to the stock market, you may want to manage part of your portfolio actively until you build up your knowledge and confidence level. For example, if you have $50,000 to invest, you may want to place 70 per cent in a buy and hold strategy and actively manage the other 30 per cent. As your confidence and knowledge increases, you would increase the amount being actively managed over time, while still maintaining a maximum of twelve stocks.

Trader

Unlike the passive or active investor, a trader is someone who treats trading more like a business than a hobby. They have a well-developed, written plan for success, and the knowledge and experience to implement it. They are able to assess market conditions using their proven trading plan and they stick to their trading rules by keeping their psychology in check and making disciplined decisions. And, they always use sound money management rules.

The frequency of trading or the amount of capital they possess are not considerations. Rather, it is the process that the trader employs to profit from the market that is important. Indeed, a trader will quite often spend as much time developing and refining their process, regardless of the timeframe or instrument being traded, as they do actually trading the market.

A proficient trader will possess the skill to trade stocks out to the top 150, or trade highly leveraged markets, confident in the knowledge that they will consistently take profits from the market.

For some of you, this will blow the stereotype of a trader out the door, as many who already invest in the stock market consider themselves a trader simply because they buy and sell stocks. The reality is that unless you have a proven process coupled with a disciplined approach that delivers consistently profitable results, year in, year out, you are deceiving yourself.

That said, whether you choose to be a passive or active investor or a proficient trader, you will come to discover that smaller portfolios with holdings concentrated in solid blue chip stocks will deliver more profitable results.

How to select the best stocks for your portfolio

So, how do you select the best stocks to place in your portfolio? Two methods that have proven very valuable for both professionals and investors alike are fundamental and technical analysis. Fundamental analysis is simply value investing, or using information to ascertain which stocks are undervalued in relation to the current price. Technical analysis, on the other hand, involves analysing charts to discern patterns in the behaviour of a stock. While many have a preference for using one form of analysis over the other, I tend to use both. I find it helps narrow down the selection of stocks to a very manageable level.

Remember, selecting the right stocks for your portfolio will depend on the time you have available, as well as your level of knowledge and skill.

Selecting stocks using fundamental analysis

When researching a company to buy shares, the three areas of fundamental analysis I primarily focus on include:

- The dividend yield of the company;
- The price earnings ratio (PE ratio);
- The earnings per share (EPS).

Dividend yield of the company

The dividend yield is simply the income you receive from holding the stock expressed as a percentage of its current market price. The dividend yield equals:

- Annual dividends per share / Current share price x 100

For example, if a stock were priced at $1.00 and was paying a dividend of $0.10, its dividend yield would be:

- $0.10 / $1.00 x 100 = 10%

When you purchase a stock, you secure the price at which the dividend yield is calculated because it is based on the price you pay for the stock. For example, if you paid $1.00 per share and the dividend paid was ten cents per share, your yield would be 10 per cent. If the price of the stock rises to $2.00 and it still pays ten cents per share, the dividend yield would represent 5 per cent, but your dividend yield would continue to be 10 per cent because you purchased the shares at $1.00.

As the price of a stock falls, its dividend yield rises and, therefore, becomes more attractive to investors seeking dividends for income. Some would have you believe that a high dividend yield means the stock is inexpensive and, therefore, an opportunity for investors to achieve good capital gains. But what this really means is that the stock has fallen to such an extent that the dividend yield is now much more attractive.

Investors, in general, don't want high-risk investments, yet, this is exactly what they get when they buy a stock that is falling in price just to receive a high dividend yield. Therefore, I would not recommend investing on dividends alone. The stock must represent good value, first and foremost, in terms of capital gains. In other words, you should look for undervalued stocks that are likely to achieve solid growth in terms of capital gains and a good income in the future.

On the whole, stocks that have a history of paying good dividends are profitable. Therefore, eventually, the price of the stock will stop falling and start to rise. Searching for securities that pay good or above average dividends may alert you to stocks that are about to turn from a long-term downtrend.

PE ratio and EPS

The potential for a company's share price to rise and fall depends on how fast its earnings are expected to grow. Therefore, the PE ratio provides investors with an indication of the prospects of the company. A low PE ratio compared to other stocks in the sector or index suggests that the stock is undervalued and a good buy. Inversely, a high PE ratio indicates that the stock is overvalued and should be sold. But this method does have its limitations; the published PE is based on the previous year's earnings, which is an historical measure rather than a projected measure of the performance of the company.

Therefore, while the PE ratio is important, I would suggest that the EPS is more so. The EPS indicates the profitability of a company. Obviously, you want to see a company deliver results, as this leads to the stock's price rising. If the EPS is consistently increasing, it suggests that the company is well managed. You also want to look at the projected EPS to see whether the growth, and, therefore, the growth of the share price, is expected to continue.

Sources of fundamental information

So where do you get fundamental information? Often, major newspapers will provide this information, as well as most online brokers. Once you find a suitable source of information, you should filter the stocks by identifying those that pay a good dividend yield, have a low PE and have a history of delivering good EPS growth.

Do not get bogged down in detail—if you find a stock has a good dividend yield and a history of delivering good EPS growth, but it does not have a low PE, I would still place this on your watch list. Similarly, if a stock has a high PE, pays little or no dividend but the stock price is rising, I would still place this on your watch list, as this could indicate a good growth stock.

A good example is BHP, which is one of the world's largest mining companies and one of the best growth stocks on the ASX. It pays below average dividends and, at times, its PE is well above the market average. However, if its projected earnings were good, I would not miss an opportunity to buy this stock. So, if a stock has a high PE, always check the dividend yield and the price of the stock before discarding it. You don't want to miss a good opportunity on a great growth stock.

The idea is to filter those stocks that are at the end of a long-term downtrend and potentially about to turn, so the parameters I mention are not hard and fast rules but rather guidelines as to how you might filter stocks.

Another area also worth investigating is company announcements. These can be a great source of information and alert you to possible changes in a stock. There is no need to read all the announcements, but you should pay particular attention to announcements about a change in a director's interest, a trading halt, the quarterly or half-yearly reports, share buyback schemes and special dividends—all of which are freely available on the stock exchange.

Selecting stocks using technical analysis

Unfortunately, many shy away from technical analysis because they believe it is overwhelmingly complex. What I want to demonstrate to you here is that using it in its simplest form can be a very powerful technique for filtering stocks. There are those in the industry who ridicule this form of analysis, believing it is of little or no value. But the information you gain from simply looking at a chart can tell you whether the stock is rising or falling in value. In other words, it provides a clear representation of the overall trend of the stock. You do not see this looking at the fundamentals of a company.

The financial industry has, for years, advocated that it is *time in the market* which is most important when it comes to investing, rather than *timing the market* to arrive at the most suitable position to buy or sell. In my opinion, accepting that time in the market is more important than timing the market explains why many achieve mediocre returns over the long term.

Markets will always rise and fall, however, the basic tenets of making superior gains remains the same. A perfect example of this is the famed investor Warren Buffett. His reliance on the methodology of "value investing" remains unwavering, even though the markets have moved from boom to bust over the decades that he has headed Berkshire Hathaway. His steadfast investing principle of buying great companies for a steal has allowed him to achieve the status of one of the world's richest men. Contrary to what you may be thinking, he too "times" his entry into investments.

Despite what the industry may advise, it really is quite easy for individuals to make superior returns from the market if they know direction—and this can be ascertained using technical analysis. However, before we move into defining how you can identify the direction of the market, let's take a look at how you can profit from human sentiment, which effectively *determines* the direction of a stock or market.

Understanding market moods

When chatting to people about the stock market, it becomes apparent that most believe market movements are caused by news or political events. However, truth be told, it is actually the social mood, or the general mood of a society, that determines direction. Would it surprise you to know that much of the news and political events that unfold are already factored into the price of the market? Let me explain.

In simple terms, social mood is about confidence, or how confident we are as a society about our future.

Experts on social mood say that a major market index is to social mood what a barometer is to weather. A barometer measures changes in the air pressure to highlight when we can expect a change in the weather. Imagine what it would mean if you were able to read the market that way! You can, and we show you how later in this chapter.

Social mood is not a study of short-term emotion but, rather, medium to long-term trends in our behaviour. To look at social moods in the short term would be just as futile as looking at the daily price movements on the stock market. Professionals know that daily fluctuations are irrelevant. Unfortunately, many individuals analyse the market this way and, in doing so, miss the bigger picture (or, in other words, the trend), which makes them far less effective.

A great example of how social mood works occurred when the Federal Reserve (or the Fed as they are known) in the United States (US) announced that it would taper quantitative easing, which is a monetary policy that simultaneously injects liquidity into the economy while reducing interest rates. Initially, the market reacted swiftly to the news with a sell-off, however, the social mood in the US at the time was more optimistic about the future, so the market quickly recovered. This repeated itself each time the Fed met to discuss the policy. It is the underlying social confidence of a market that determines direction, not short-term emotions.

The more confident the underlying social mood, the more likely we are to invest. The more pessimistic it is, the more likely we are to sell out of the market. Understanding the collective mood of a society is easier than trying to keep up with the latest in world economics and news events, then trying to understand how this may impact your investments (which is even harder). It also ensures that you are better prepared for the most important moves in the market.

There is a point in any trend when the social mood becomes overly optimistic or overly pessimistic. This occurs around market tops and bottoms, signalling a likely change in trend. Unfortunately, the masses tend to miss these signals and, instead, get caught out buying at the top and selling at the bottom of a market, behaviour prevalent during the GFC. Being aware of the social mood means that you won't get swept up in the mindset of the herd.

Analysing direction

Looking at the direction in which a stock is trending is probably the simplest, most direct way to decide which stocks to buy and sell. Imagine, for a moment, you are in France and you want to get on a train to go to Italy. Obviously, if the next train that pulls into the station is heading to Italy, you would hop on and enjoy the ride. But what if, after you embarked on the journey, you discovered the train wasn't heading to Italy but, instead, going to Spain? No doubt you would get off the train at the next available station and wait until another train that was heading to Italy came your way. And so it is with stocks—if a stock is trending up, you want to get on the train and go with the flow. But if it is trending down, you want to get off and wait for the next stock that is trending up.

When prices rise for a period of time and then fall away, a crest or peak is formed. On the other hand, when prices fall for a period of time and then rise once again, they form a low, or what is more commonly known as a trough. Therefore, an uptrend is the result of a rising movement in market prices, which is confirmed by a series of higher peaks and troughs. Meanwhile, a downtrend is caused by a falling movement in market prices, and is confirmed by a series of lower peaks and troughs.

A rising stock is said to be bullish, as shown in Figure 4.1, opposite, indicating there are more buyers than sellers, while a falling stock is said to be bearish, as shown in Figure 4.2, opposite, indicating there are more sellers than buyers.

Figure 4.1: Bullish or upward trending market

Figure 4.2: Bearish or downward trending market

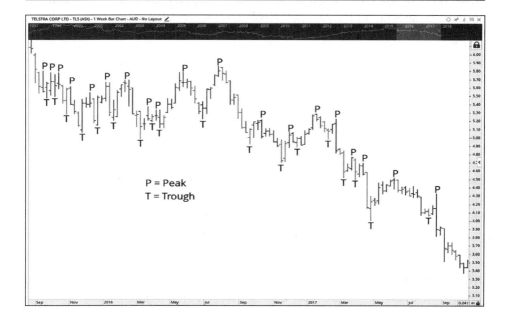

A major consideration when investing over the long term is the direction of the trend over the longer term and, to a lesser extent, the medium term. Given this, you will gauge a lot of what you need to know by analysing the trends of a stock on a monthly chart.

If, however, you are trading over the medium term, the major consideration is the direction of the trend over the medium term and, to a lesser extent, the shorter term. Given this, you will gauge a lot of what you need to know by analysing the trends of a stock on a weekly and monthly chart.

The major consideration when investing over the short term is the direction of the trend over the medium term; therefore, you will gauge a lot of what you need to know by analysing the trends of a stock on a weekly chart. That said, it still pays to confirm the longer-term trend by reviewing the monthly chart. Remember, just as the train from France to Italy may stop, start or even be delayed or diverted, it will eventually end up in Italy. By reviewing the monthly chart, you will be able to gauge the direction, the length and the strength of each trend of lesser degree.

When viewing a chart, you will be able to tell that the price of a stock is rising if it has successively higher bars. On a monthly chart, stocks that rise over three or more consecutive months are said to be in an uptrend. On a weekly chart, this equates to twelve or more bars moving in an uptrend. Obviously, this statement is not flawless, as a stock can rise for three months (or twelve weeks) and then move sideways or down. However, it does provide a starting point from which you can analyse the strength of a stock. Let's look at some examples.

The monthly chart of Aristocrat Leisure, in Figure 4.3, opposite, represents the stock as it rose in price from 2003 to 2017, where the trend changed from up to down before returning to trade in an uptrend again. In effect, it represents the consensus of thousands of investors over a period of fourteen consecutive years as the stock trended up from $0.75 to $17.68, then down to $2.10 before rising back up to $22.40.

Depending on your confidence level, you might have entered the stock some time late in 2003 after it had been trending up for more than three consecutive months. But even if you had waited until sometime in early 2004, when the price of the stock was approximately $2.70, you would still have made around 360 per cent, excluding dividends, before selling in 2007 at a point where the stock had fallen more than 30 per cent in price, using very conservative entry and exit rules.

Not every stock will give you this sort of profit, but most blue chip companies usually yield around 20 to 50 per cent or more in growth in an uptrend. As you can see on the chart, we placed the next entry in 2012 at $3.25 based on the same rules and, again, the profit is quite impressive.

Figure 4.3: Aristocrat Leisure 2003 to 2017

So what is the monthly chart of Westpac, Figure 4.4, below, telling you?

Figure 4.4: Westpac 1992 to 2017

Once again, this is representative of a solid blue chip stock that has trended up nicely between late 1992 and 2017, by over 1,200 per cent, excluding dividends.

While there have been many opportunities to profit from this stock over the past 25 years, with the stock rising between twenty to 50 per cent or more over a few months to around three years, I have shown one trade using the same simple rules I applied in Figure 4.3, above, with the trade making just over 40 per cent in two years. Generally, the top fifty stocks by market capitalisation produce very steady uptrends that are easy to identify. Stocks out to the top 150, however, are a little more volatile and, therefore, require more diligence on your part if you choose to invest in them.

As with any stock, there is always an element of risk, but the educated investor can minimise this risk. Remember, you can always sell if you are wrong in your analysis.

If you decide to use technical analysis, you will need to access services that provide the facility to view charts. Fortunately, there are many websites that now provide this service for free, eliminating the need for you to purchase expensive software. In addition, some websites also allow you to select and monitor stocks of interest to you. Most online brokers also provide access to stock charts on their websites.

The million dollar mistake

To assist you in understanding why it is so important to trade with the trend, I want to share with you a story that could one day make you millions.

Imagine you are driving in a fog, without any fog lights. Visibility is poor and you can only see a couple of metres in front of you. You are on edge, your palms sweaty, your muscles tense and your breathing laboured, as you watch for any movement on the side of the road or in front of you. Corners come about fast, you are breaking a lot and, at times, you just want to stop the car and get out.

However, the problem isn't the fog; it's the fact that you have no idea what lies ahead. Whether or not you've actually experienced this, you can imagine how stressful this situation would be.

Unfortunately, this is how many individuals trade the stock market, particularly those starting out, but also those who have been trading for some time but don't have the right knowledge and skill.

Just like driving in the fog, people often have little or no idea what lies ahead, or how to manage themselves when conditions become rough. Because of this, many struggle with a fear of the unknown and so repeat the same mistakes of entering or exiting a trade at the wrong time.

When you first enter a trade, you don't know anything for certain, except maybe how you are going to manage the trade as it unfolds. This is why it is important to always have a solid understanding of the stock before you decide to enter, as you could be trading on the edge of a cliff or, in other words, a stock that is in a long decline.

A few years ago, a client who had just commenced studying with us shared how he had mixed results in his trading. What I am about to share with you changed the way he thought about trading, and changed his fortune. During an initial discussion, I asked him a simple question: "When you enter a trade, how well do you see what's really going on?"

Unfortunately, many struggle to answer this question, as most don't see what's right in front of them until it's too late. This is one of the main reasons why the majority who attempt to trade only last around six months, or maybe a couple of years, before they drop out. Eventually, the market weeds out those who persist in making the same mistakes over and over.

The client had been trading a million-dollar portfolio and he told me that he had been trading for years but with mixed success. He wanted to start from the ground up. He had previously been using moving averages and other lagging indicators he had learned about at different seminars and in internet research.

On his first day in our course, he sent me a chart of a trade he had taken. He wanted to know what he did wrong. It was a daily chart of Cochlear (COH). Figure 4.5, overleaf, shows where he entered the trade in 2011, when the stock was trading at $75.02, as he had identified that this was an important resistance level. Before entering the trade, he had done one thing right, which was to set a stop loss; he was prepared to risk less than 7 per cent of his capital in the trade.

Figure 4.5: Daily chart of Cochlear

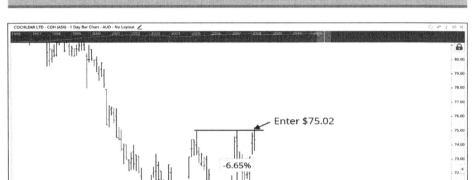

Initially, the stock rose by around 3.3 per cent, as shown in Figure 4.6, opposite, before falling heavily (I have removed the analysis from the chart so that it is easy to read).

As the stock fell away, the client was stopped out at around 20 per cent below his buy price, as the stock gapped down. So, on a position size of $100,000, he had suffered a 20 per cent, or $20,000 loss. Ouch! He also mentioned that he had been stopped out a number of other times, all with big losses.

The million-dollar question isn't whether he should have set a tighter stop loss. The point is that he should never have been in the trade in the first place.

Figure 4.6: Daily chart of Cochlear with falling share price

So, let's review what the client should have considered before entering the trade. Figure 4.7, overleaf, shows the weekly chart of COH. At the time the client entered the stock on the daily chart, there was no entry on the weekly chart, as it had been falling for eighteen weeks just prior to his entry. This demonstrates how being too focused on the short term and not understanding the bigger picture can kill your opportunity to take millions from the market.

Figure 4.7: Weekly chart of Cochlear

The point is that, regardless of what you are trading or the intended timeframe, it is always important to look at the next larger timeframe to understand the landscape you are trading in. Furthermore, you need to ensure you have solid rules and analysis behind your decision to trade. This shows you understand the risk you are taking and know when to enter or exit.

Looking at the monthly chart of COH, Figure 4.8, opposite, you can see that at the time the client entered the trade, the stock appeared to be reversing direction, as indicated by the outside (last) bar. In reality, however, price was still technically falling in a downtrend and there was no confirmation that the trend was changing, only speculation that it might, which in my book, is gambling. This made what the client was doing very high risk.

Had the client analysed the stock with the right knowledge, he would have found many reasons not to take the trade.

It really does pay to know the terrain you are trading in before taking a trade. This means you are more likely to enter at a safer, lower risk point in time, and you are, therefore, more likely to profit.

Figure 4.8: Monthly chart of Cochlear

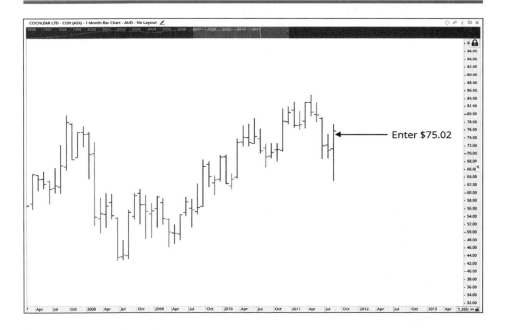

Enter $75.02

Diversification

Before moving on, I want to ensure you understand the advantages and disadvantages of this much-talked about investment technique as it pertains to investing in international markets. Your understanding of diversification will determine the profitability of your portfolio and your success in the stock market.

In Chapter 1, I alluded to the fact that many in the industry suggest that you should diversify within asset classes in order to reduce the risk of your investment portfolio and increase returns. Some also argue that investing in international markets can lower risk without sacrificing returns. However, it's important to understand that this is a gimmick that will cost you dearly over the long term.

In Australia, the industry's catchcry for suggesting that you diversify into international equities rests on the fact that the Australian market represents less than 2 per cent of global markets. According to the "experts", this means most investment opportunities are available offshore. Similar catchcries exist in other markets. For example, in the US, many major institutions claim international stocks have outperformed US stocks over the long term. To substantiate this claim, they present selected timeframes in an attempt to convince investors.

But this raises a question: If you can't make money in your own backyard, why would you consider investing in international equities? You only have to watch a child in a lolly shop to know that more choice leads to confusion and overwhelm, and neither is a good state to be in when trading the stock market. In my book, we're really talking about di-worsification.

You not only have to contend with market risk in another country, which requires more knowledge, time and skill, but also the fluctuations in exchange rates, which have the potential to worsen returns—particularly if the dollar is appreciating against the other currency. Why would anyone consider diversifying their portfolio to take on more market risk, let alone the additional costs associated with investing in international equities?

The industry further substantiates its support for diversifying into international equities by suggesting that this asset class outperforms other asset classes over the longer term. However, the majority of institutions also diversify their portfolio into cash and bonds, which underperform equities and property by a considerable margin over the longer term. Consequently, cash and bonds pull down the overall performance of a fund. Given this, it would seem that while diversification was devised as a way to minimise risk, many in the financial services industry also use it as a way to reduce profits.

Research conducted by Fidelity International on thirty years of investment returns further substantiates my argument that global diversification is detrimental to your portfolio. Table 4.1, below, shows the growth of $10,000 over the past thirty years to December 2016 for Australian and global shares. The returns represent the average annual return and assume all dividends have been reinvested.

Table 4.1: 30 years in Australian and global shares		
Financial asset	**Australia**	**Global**
Shares	9.10% p.a.	7.00% p.a.

No doubt some of you may be thinking that if you reside outside of Australia, it would make sense to diversify your portfolio into Australian stocks to take advantage of the higher returns offered. However, this view is contradicted by an article produced by Owen[4] in Australia, which compared the total return (with all dividends reinvested) from investing in the Australian stock market versus the US stock market, after taking into account inflation (but before taxation and broking costs), from 1900 to the end of 2017. In other words, it compared the total return from the All Ordinaries Index in Australian dollars after Australian CPI inflation versus the total returns for the S&P 500 index in US dollars after US CPI inflation.

Interestingly, the article demonstrates that the total return for Australian investors has been virtually the same as for American investors (in local markets, taking into account currencies and inflation). The return on investment from both markets averaged around 6.60 per cent, in real terms, over 117 years.

Although the total returns were the same, there were large differences for long periods of time as Australia and the US took turns at having bigger booms and subsequent bigger busts, as shown in Figure 4.9, overleaf. But as I have previously stated, why would anyone want to contend with the higher risks, let alone higher costs, of investing in another country when the benefits of operating a concentrated portfolio in their own country are so much greater?

Don't be fooled by the clichés marketed by the institutions. Often, those promoting them are focused on lining their own pockets—not yours.

Figure 4.9: Real returns from shares—Australia versus USA since 1900

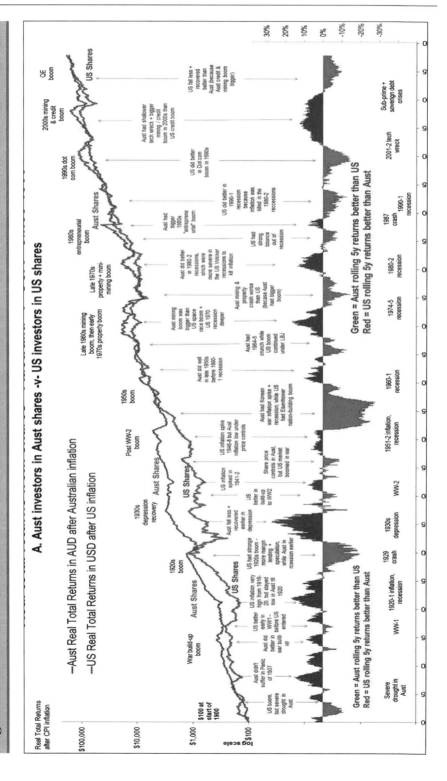

Building a portfolio

In Chapter 3, I introduced you to a simple methodology for developing a list of stocks, or a watch list, to suit the goal of your portfolio. But how do you filter your watch list to identify the best stocks to buy when building a portfolio?

My intention in this section is to show you how you can develop a set of simple rules to filter down your selection of stocks. In doing so, we will construct a portfolio from the top twenty stocks listed on the ASX. Later, in Chapter 6, we will trade the portfolio to show you how you can confidently profit from investing in a concentrated portfolio, without the need to dilute returns with over-diversification.

Table 4.2, overleaf, lists the top twenty stocks on the ASX as at 31 December 2006. The intention is to construct a blue chip portfolio over the long term to deliver growth and income. Because fundamental data from 2007 is harder to come by, I have chosen to filter the stocks based on the following rules:

- The stock must be in an uptrend for at least three months and be at or above its all-time high price; and

- The dividend yield for the stock must be 3 per cent or greater.

Stock Name	Code	Trending up for at least 3 months	At or above previous high	Dividend yield
AMP	AMP	Yes	No	8%
ANZ Bank	ANZ	Yes	Yes	2%
BHP	BHP	No	No	1%
Brambles	BXB	Yes	Yes	-
Commonwealth Bank	CBA	Yes	Yes	5%
CSL Ltd	CSL	Yes	Yes	3%
Fosters Group	FGL	Yes	Yes	4%
Macquarie Group	MQG	Yes	Yes	3%
National Australia Bank	NAB	Yes	Yes	4%
QBE Insurance	QBE	Yes	Yes	3%
Rio Tinto	RIO	No	No	1%
St George Bank	SGB	Yes	Yes	5%
Stockland	SGP	Yes	Yes	5%
Suncorp Metway	SUN	Yes	No	3%
Telstra	TLS	Yes	No	3%
Wesfarmers	WES	Yes	No	4%
Westfield	WDC	Yes	Yes	7%
Westpac Bank	WBC	Yes	No	3%
Woodside Petroleum	WPL	No	No	1%
Woolworths	WOW	Yes	Yes	2%

Table 4.2: Top 20 ASX stocks as at 31 December 2006

After analysing all twenty stocks, I identified nine stocks that met the selection criteria. For the purposes of this example, we will invest $100,000 and assume brokerage costs of $25 or 0.1 per cent per trade, whichever is the greater, through an online broker. Given that we need to minimise our exposure to risk, no more than 20 per cent of the capital will be invested in any one stock. The stocks purchased on market opening on the ASX on 2 January 2007 are listed in Table 4.3, below, with all prices adjusted for corporate actions.

Table 4.3: Stocks purchased on the ASX on 2 January 2007

Stock code	Buy price	No. of shares	Amount	Total amount[1]
CBA	$49.12	225	$11,052.00	$11,077.00
CSL	$21.67	511	$11,073.37	$11,098.37
FGL	$5.67	1955	$11,084.85	$11,109.85
MQG	$77.80	142	$11,047.60	$11,072.60
NAB	$38.49	288	$11,085.12	$11,110.12
QBE	$28.07	394	$11,059.58	$11,084.58
SGB	$32.97	336	$11,077.92	$11,102.92
SGP	$7.87	1408	$11,080.96	$11,105.96
WDC	$10.48	1057	$11,077.36	$11,102.36

1. After brokerage costs of $25 or 0.1% per transaction, whichever is greater

While you would normally construct your portfolio over time as opportunities arise, I want to demonstrate how powerful the techniques and strategies are that I outline in this book. Therefore, I have decided to commence the portfolio from 2 January, just prior to the GFC, which was the worst time to be in the stock market since the crash in 1987 when the stock market fell 50 per cent in price over seven weeks. In comparison, the market fell just over 50 per cent in seventy-one weeks during the GFC.

Would it surprise you to know that 1973-1974 was the biggest bust in the history of the Australian stock market? The market fell around 60 per cent, which is technically considered a crash. It's only because it fell over many years that many did not view it that way.

Remember, concentrated portfolios tend to perform better, so I recommend you hold no more than 5 to 8 stocks (although, depending on the goal of your portfolio, you may choose to hold up to twelve stocks). Keep in mind, holding more than twelve stocks will dilute your returns and increase the risks you are taking.

If, after analysing a number of stocks, you identify fewer than five opportunities to buy, I recommend you only purchase these stocks and wait until other opportunities arise. It is far better to stay safe and keep your money in the bank than to risk buying stocks that don't have a high probability of rising.

To reiterate, simply by looking at the chart of a stock, you can identify whether it is rising in an uptrend. In most cases, you will see short-term fluctuations in the trend of a stock, but if it has been trending up, there is a very high probability it will continue to rise.

In the case of Telstra, in Figure 4.10, below, the stock completed a long-term downtrend before reversing direction and commencing a new uptrend in 2010, with an entry created at $3.00 in May 2011. As you can see, the stock continued trending up for approximately five years before changing trend.

Figure 4.10: Telstra 2008 to 2017

As shown in Figure 4.11, below, Macquarie Group reversed direction in 2011 before commencing a new uptrend, with an opportunity to enter at $29.68 in October 2012. It then continued up for over five years and, as you can see, the stock is still unfolding in a longer-term uptrend.

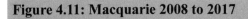

Figure 4.11: Macquarie 2008 to 2017

To sum up

Remember, it is not how much money you make on any investment that makes you wealthy, it is how much you do not lose over time. This is why it is so important to ensure you are trading with the longer-term direction of a stock or market. Getting this right, means you can pinpoint with greater certainty, the right time to buy or sell.

Using fundamental analysis in combination with technical analysis will enable you to filter the best stocks to place in your portfolio. Although, remember, the higher the return you desire, the more knowledge, experience and time you will need to devote to your investments.

You also need to ensure you don't over diversify. Therefore, I recommend holding no more than 5 to 8 stocks, although depending on the goal of your portfolio, you may want to hold up to twelve. Concentrated portfolios that are managed wisely tend to perform much better over the longer term.

Now that you understand how to narrow down the selection of stocks to place on your watch list, let's investigate how to buy and sell stocks to manage your portfolio.

Chapter 5

How to Be Trendy

"I don't set trends. I just find out what they are and exploit them."

Dick Clark

No doubt some of you will have heard that trends represent the basic foundation of trading any market. Sayings such as "the trend is your friend" and "always trade with the trend" are common place in books or courses about trading. The 90 per cent of individuals who lose money in the markets today do so because they unknowingly break from this basic foundation of trading by trading counter to the trend.

The carved-in-stone rule you must always remember is this: All trends conform to a longer-term, existing trend.

For example, if a stock has been in a long-term downtrend for two years, there is a high probability it will continue to fall; in fact, the probability is as high as 80 to 90 per cent. If after falling for two years, the stock then turns and rises for five weeks, the probability that it is starting a new uptrend is only 10 to 20 per cent. Unfortunately, at this point in time, many people fall into the trap of believing a new uptrend is unfolding, and they attempt to buy at the bottom for fear of missing out on the potential rise. The cold reality is that, often, the market turns down again, causing the individual to suffer more losses. Acting on this low probability of a potential change in trend is not conducive to good trading. You should always trade with the trend.

In the previous chapter, we introduced you to a simple concept for analysing the direction of the market. In order to trade these trends, it is important to understand how bull and bear markets unfold and, more importantly, how to recognise the start and end of a trend.

Mastering direction

Charles Dow, the man who established the Dow Jones Industrial Average in 1896, was arguably one of the first analysts to truly define the commonalities found in bull and bear markets. He discovered that certain measurable trends evolved over time. Unfortunately he passed away before he was able to quantify and publish his full findings. However, a number of Dow's associates combined his various workings into what we know today as Dow Theory. So let's review how you can use this theory to your advantage in determining market direction.

A trend is a movement in price either up, down or sideways that can take place over weeks, months or even years, and all trends can be traded profitably. According to Dow Theory, there are three types of trends in the market:

- A primary trend, either bull or bear, which may take place over several years;

- Secondary movements or reactions, which usually take place over many weeks or months and run contrary to the primary trend; and

- Daily fluctuations, which can move in either direction (bull or bear).

Figure 5.1, opposite, indicates the three different types of movements in the market.

Figure 5.1: Trends according to Dow Theory

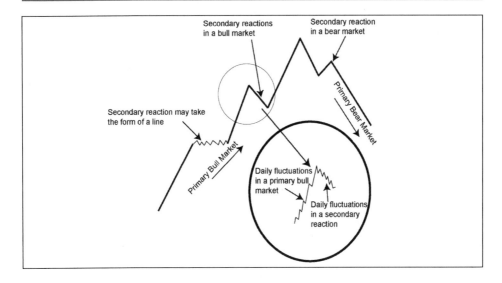

Primary trends

The primary movements are the principal focus of Dow Theory. Each primary trend, whether bull or bear, encompasses three phases which reflect the market behaviour we are trying to identify, as shown in Figure 5.2, below

Figure 5.2: Bull and bear market phases

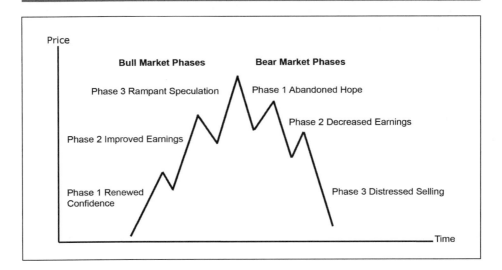

Secondary movements or reactions

The secondary movements in Figure 5.1, on page 69, consist of a downward movement in a bull market and an upward movement in a bear market. Secondary movements may take the form of a line, which indicates either an accumulation pattern (which takes place at market bottoms or during an uptrend) or a distribution pattern (which takes place at market tops or during a downtrend). A line is a price movement over several weeks or longer. Breakouts above the line indicate accumulation and forecast higher prices, while breakouts below the line imply distribution and that lower prices will follow.

Daily fluctuations

According to Dow Theory, daily fluctuations are not significant in determining the primary trend of the market and should, therefore, be ignored. This view is, in fact, contrary to what is taught in modern technical analysis, given that many courses and books promote the use of daily charts to analyse the market. Unfortunately, this is one of the main reasons why many individuals are not profitable. Analysing monthly charts to determine the primary trend and weekly charts to fine-tune your entry and exit points will inevitably make you far more profitable. So let's look at how you analyse trends in the market according to Dow Theory.

Figure 5.3, opposite, is a weekly chart of the All Ordinaries Index (XAO). Note that I have marked several areas where the relative phases of the market appear to have completed and the current phase that looks to resemble "rampant speculation". As we are using a weekly chart in this example, it is important to understand that the analysis only reflects the short to medium view, which is up to around eighteen months, although this is not a hard and fast rule. Later, I will share the longer-term view on the monthly chart.

Figure 5.3: Phases of the market—weekly chart of XAO

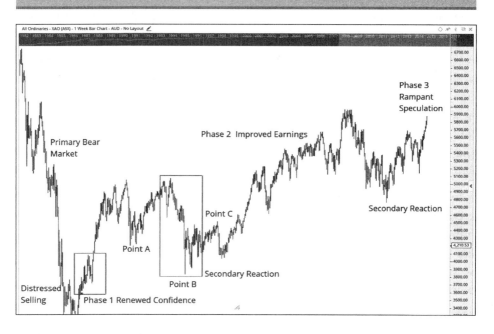

Let's look at each section in more detail. The GFC and subsequent major low into March 2009 was the end of a primary bear market. As Dow observed, the final phase of the primary bear market is distressed selling; all of those who hadn't yet sold would have given up hope of a return to higher prices and started to exit the market. This can be seen in the chart above, with the sharp fall over eight weeks into November 2008. The market rose slightly for seven weeks in a secondary reaction prior to its final fall into the March 2009 low nine weeks later.

Around this time, educated investors would have been preparing to re-enter the market. But how would they know the right time to enter?

Part of Dow's research involved determining the patterns that signalled the end of one primary trend and the start of another. In the case of the start of a new upward trend, Dow observed: "A new upward trend will be confirmed when the market doesn't move to a consecutively lower low and high."

In other words, a new upward trend is confirmed by higher lows and higher highs. The opposite is true in a bear market, where a new downtrend is confirmed by lower highs and lower lows. It is the understanding of this simple insight that separates successful investors from the not so successful. If you recognise the beginning of a new trend, you will be in a far better position to profit from a trade and your results will improve dramatically.

In Figure 5.3, on page 71, I have marked the first instance where a higher low was confirmed (first box) following the 2009 low, which indicated that the market was returning to an upward trend. This could also be considered the start of the first phase in a new primary bull market—"increased confidence".

A secondary reaction into the 2011 low (Point B, second box) followed the peak of the first phase in April of the same year. Notice how this low took out the prior significant low at Point A. Some may have taken this to be a return to a primary bear market given the significance of the pull back. However, the accumulation into Point C (notice again the consistently higher lows and highs during this smaller run up) indicated that a return to higher prices was likely. Smart investors would have seen this and begun buying top quality stocks.

As we can see, the market traded significantly higher over the next few years, breaking the April 2011 high and travelling in what appears to be Phase 2 of the primary bull market—"improved earnings". The high in April 2015 was possibly the top of Phase 2, as the market fell into February 2016 in what looks like a secondary phase. This implies that we should see a third phase in the bull market before moving into the next bear market.

The market moved up strongly from the low in February 2016 in what seems likely to be Phase 3 of a bull market—"rampant speculation". That said, remember we have used a weekly chart in this example. It is important to remember that all movements in a market are only movements of lesser degree of the larger trend. Given this, the upward move since March 2009 is likely to be Phase 1 of a much larger move, as shown on the monthly chart, Figure 5.4, opposite.

Figure 5.4: Phases of the market—monthly chart of XAO

Trading with the trend

While trading is a science, it is also an art form where probability and risk are assessed with each trade taken. While it is important to always trade with the trend, if a trader were to always wait for the long-term trend to confirm, many low risk trades would be missed. Therefore, it is important to remember that trends unfold with the short-term trend confirming first, followed by the medium-term trend and, finally, the long-term trend.

This means, while it is important to always trade with the trend, a medium-term investor would look to enter a trade at the earliest possible point prior to the short and medium-term trend confirming. But how do you identify when an uptrend is about to start or when a downtrend is about to finish so as to enter the trend at the earliest possible time?

Trading the trend

Trend lines are one of the oldest and most effective methods for deciding which stocks to buy and sell, yet, they are one of the most underutilised tools. Why? The answer is simply lack of knowledge—many investors do not understand how a trend forms or how it unfolds over time. Once you understand this concept, you will become far more profitable.

In theory, using trend lines is very simple—buy when a stock crosses above a downtrend line and sell when a stock crosses below an uptrend line. This can be done, quite simply, by applying a pencil and ruler to a chart. The major advantage of using trend lines is that they can indicate when a trend may be changing before confirmation of the actual change in trend is evident.

In effect, trend lines measure the rate of change in the price of a stock, which allows you to determine the momentum of the buyers and sellers. In other words, they provide a very visual representation of the limits of the buyers and sellers. If the momentum of a stock increases from the prevailing side in a trend, the rate at which the price changes increases as well.

For example, in an uptrend if there are more buyers than sellers, this will push the price of a stock up; if a lot of buyers suddenly start to buy the stock, the price will increase more rapidly. The steepness of the trend will also increase, meaning you need to follow this move with your trend line. Let's take a closer look.

Drawing downtrend lines

A downtrend line is used to identify when you would enter a stock that is rising in value. To begin, you need to define the parameters of the current trend. Remember, if you are trading over the longer term, you would do this on a monthly chart, however, if trading over the medium to short term, you would do this on a weekly chart. It is important to note that a trend must exist before you can draw a trend line. In other words, you need to see consistently lower peaks and troughs for a downtrend to exist.

To begin drawing your trend line, you would start at the highest peak in price and then look for successively lower peaks and troughs. You should be able to identify from this that the stock is trending down. Next, you simply draw a line across the peaks of the downtrend. For a trend line to be considered valid, you always require three peaks on a downtrend; two peaks is considered an unconfirmed trend line.

Also be aware that your trend line does not have to touch each of the three peaks; each peak can be slightly above or below the trend line, although they should never be more than a few per cent away from the line. Figure 5.5, opposite, is an example of how you would draw a valid downtrend line.

When a stock is below the line, you should not own it; it is in a downtrend and has a high probability of falling further. However, when it breaks above the downtrend line, we know there is a high probability that the trend is changing.

Figure 5.5: Downtrend line

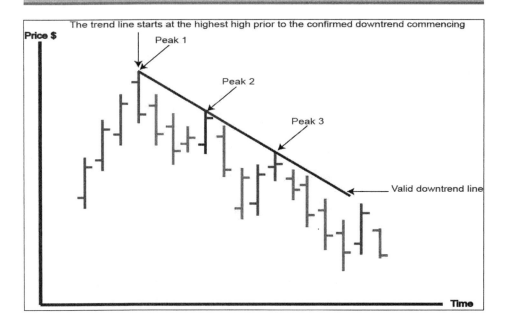

Drawing uptrend lines

The rules for drawing uptrend lines are simply the opposite of the rules for downtrend lines. An uptrend line is used to identify when you would exit a stock that is about to fall in value. Once again, you need to define the parameters of the current trend, which you would do on a monthly chart if you were trading over the long term and a weekly chart if trading over the short to medium term. Remember—you must see consistently higher peaks and troughs for an uptrend to exist. Then you can draw a valid uptrend line.

To identify the trend, you start at the lowest point prior to where the stock crossed above your last downtrend line and look for successively higher peaks and troughs. You should be able to identify from this that the stock is trending up. You will require three troughs for the uptrend line to be considered valid. Figure 5.6, overleaf, shows how you would draw a valid uptrend line.

Figure 5.6: Uptrend line

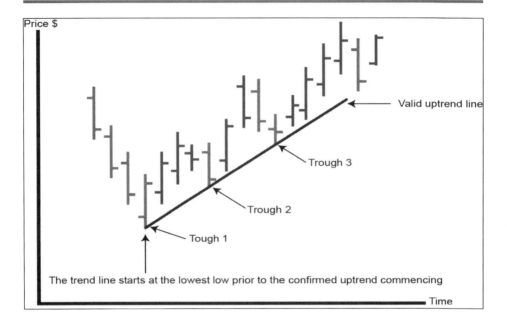

When the stock is above the uptrend line, it has a high probability of continuing its uptrend. However, when it breaks below the uptrend line you would sell, as the probability of the uptrend continuing is unlikely.

Do not get perturbed if you find you cannot accurately draw trend lines to begin with; there is room for flexibility if you get your analysis wrong. As you build your confidence over time, you will find yourself able to identify trends very easily and draw trend lines that are far more accurate.

Now that you understand how to draw trend lines, let's look at how you would use this tool to buy and sell stocks.

Buying and selling on trend lines

Depending on the timeframe you are analysing, the rules of entry for trend lines will vary. For example, if you are investing for the long term and using a monthly chart, when a stock closes once above a downtrend line, it constitutes a buy signal. Conversely, it stands to reason that when a stock closes once below an uptrend line on a monthly chart, you should sell. The closing price is defined as the price of the last trade for the month—the horizontal line on the right hand side of each bar represents the closing price. Given this, you need to look at your charts at the end of each month to filter which stocks you will buy and sell. Let's look at an example.

On the monthly chart of Insurance Australia Group, Figure 5.7, below, you can see that the downtrend line drawn from the high of January 2007 down to February 2012 clearly indicates a downtrend is in place.

The break above the trend line also indicates the start of a possible uptrend. This resulted in an opportunity to buy at $3.19 on 1 March 2012. The stock continued to rise for three years to around $6.61 before price fell below the uptrend line, triggering an exit at $6.00 and achieving a return of almost 90 per cent excluding dividends.

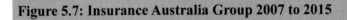

Figure 5.7: Insurance Australia Group 2007 to 2015

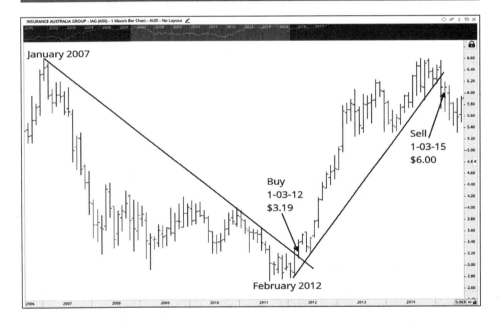

If you had analysed Brambles at the end of 2003, you would have bought the stock at around $4.91 in January 2004, when it closed once above the downtrend line on the monthly chart, as shown in Figure 5.8, overleaf.

The stock continued to rise strongly over three and half years. The uptrend line then triggered a sell at around $10.32 in August 2007, generating a profit of 110 per cent excluding dividends. After exiting, you will notice that the stock price continued to rise for another two months.

You may remember that October 2007 was the start of the GFC. After exiting, Brambles did not trigger another entry over the two months it rose. Following the high in October 2007, Brambles fell away for seventeen months into March 2009. This example, therefore, highlights two things: Firstly, that some stocks will rise after your exit rules are triggered, which is fine because you can always get back in if another entry is triggered. And secondly, that blue chip stocks will generally give you a solid exit signal prior to any significant fall.

Figure 5.8: Brambles 2001 to 2007

If you were trading over the medium term using a weekly chart, you would enter a trade when the stock had two consecutive closes above a downtrend line. Inversely, you would exit the trade when the stock had two consecutive closes below an uptrend line.

When analysing the weekly chart of Westpac, Figure 5.9, opposite, a couple of interesting points become evident. The first is that correctly placing a trend line on a weekly chart is a little more challenging, as this chart is more sensitive to price movements than the monthly chart. The second is that the trade is shorter in terms of time, which is typical when trading on a weekly chart as opposed to a monthly chart.

Figure 5.9: Westpac 2015 to 2017

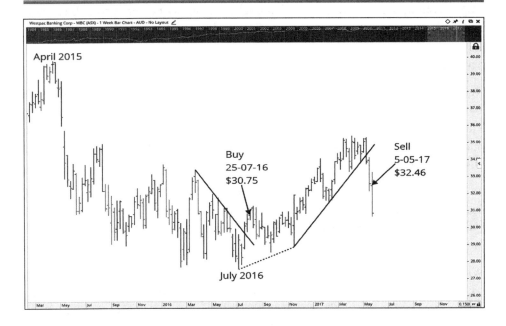

So which is more profitable? The answer really depends on your investment goals and what you are trading. I have seen monthly charts significantly outperform the gains made on weekly charts on the same stock over the same period and vice versa, which is why you should always analyse both timeframes before you trade.

As you can see on the chart above, Westpac continued to trend down from the high in April 2015 to a low in July 2016, before triggering an entry above the downtrend line in July 2016 at $30.75. The stock then traded up for around nine months before falling below the uptrend, triggering an exit in May 2017 and achieving a gain of 5.56 per cent excluding dividends.

While trend lines do provide you with a very useful analysis tool for filtering when to buy and sell stocks, they are only, on average, around 70 per cent accurate (although, this will vary with the stock you are analysing). In other words, around 30 per cent of the time, you will be wrong in your analysis. For this reason, you should always use a stop loss when investing in the stock market.

A stop loss is simply a method of protecting capital if an investment turns bad. In most cases, you would set a stop loss at 10 to 15 per cent below your buy price, depending on the volatility of the stock. For example, if you buy a stock at $10.00 and set a stop loss of 10 per cent, you would sell once the stock fell $0.01 below $9.00. Obviously, where you set your stop loss will vary depending on your tolerance to risk. That said, I recommend you never set your stop loss at less than 10 per cent when trading blue chip stocks. Otherwise, you will get stopped out of trades—some of which could potentially be very profitable. I will demonstrate how to apply stop losses in more detail in Chapter 8.

To sum up

Remember, mastering direction will ensure you are always trading with the trend. By understanding the phases of the market as they unfold according to Dow Theory, you will be in a much better position to compound the returns of your portfolio, as you will be in the market when it is the best time to profit and you will be sitting on the sidelines when the market, or a stock is in a decline.

No doubt, prior to reading this chapter, many of you would not have believed that you could make solid profits by simply applying a pencil and ruler to a chart. Using trend lines to buy and sell stocks, however, is one of the most effective methods for trading trends.

While trend lines will provide you with a very useful analysis tool for filtering when to buy and sell stocks, it is important that you always use them in combination with a stop loss as their effectiveness is only, on average, 70 per cent accurate, although this will depend on the stock you are trading. Remember, a stop loss is simply a method to protect capital if an investment turns sour. Using trend lines and stop losses will shield you from losses, so that you protect your capital and minimise the risk of losses being compounded.

Now that you understand how to recognise trends and how to buy and sell using trend lines, let's trade the portfolio we created in Chapter 4 over ten years to see what returns are achievable.

Chapter 6

Riding the Waves

"Most investors want to do today what they should have done yesterday."

Larry Summers

Learning to trade is like learning how to drive a car. Once you know how to drive, you can drive any car in the world. And so it is with the stock market; once you have the right knowledge and have proven that you can trade by consistently taking profits from the market, you can apply your knowledge to trade any market in the world.

Misguidedly, the majority of people who trade the stock market rely on technical indicators (which became prevalent with the introduction of computers) to analyse price alone or, at best, price with a little bit of pattern analysis. For the most part, technical indicators are considered lagging indicators, as they only inform you after the market has already moved. This explains why individuals who use them generally place a lot more trades, which makes the brokers more money, but results in you achieving very mediocre returns.

So, if computers are not increasing the probability of achieving consistently profitable returns from the stock market, what can? Quite simply, to be consistently successful in trading, you need to do what the 10 per cent who are successful do, which is use leading indicators, such as the trend lines that I discussed in the previous chapter. These provide more consistent and often earlier entry and exit signals, resulting in more profit in your back pocket.

In my own analysis, I also use price, pattern and time because when all three areas converge at the same point on a chart, the probability of a move increases dramatically and reduces risk accordingly. Combining all three methods of analysis reduces the risk of getting caught out in false moves, which is a common problem many individuals struggle with. In essence, combining price, pattern and time increases the probability that you enter or exit a stock at the earliest possible point and at the lowest possible risk.

While the detailed application of price, pattern and time falls outside the scope of this book, I'm going to summarise how they help stack the odds in your favour.

Stacking the odds in your favour

As I have previously stated, there is an inherent level of risk involved in trading the stock market. To be consistently profitable, you need to assess whether the risk you are contemplating is worth taking. But how do you assess this risk and how do you ensure the odds are stacked in your favour?

Often, people ask, "When I have two stocks giving a buy signal, which is the best to buy?" What they are really asking is which stock will make the most amount of profit. But as I always say, trading is not about how much money you can make; it is about how much you do not lose over time. So I respond to this question by asking, "Which stock will give you the least amount of risk if you decide to trade it?" Obviously, the higher the probability of the stock giving you a winning trade, the more the odds are stacked in your favour.

Trading is not about how much money you can make; it is about how much you do not lose over time.

So let's investigate how you can stack the odds in your favour.

Price

We use price analysis to tell us the most likely price points where the change in trend will occur. We do this by analysing the entire history of the stock and finding the strongest levels of confidence in price. If the price of a stock hits a significant price level, this alerts us to the fact that there is a high probability that the market will turn. We then look to analyse pattern, to confirm the change in trend.

Pattern

Pattern analysis alerts us to the emotions of the buyers and sellers and tells us whether the buyers or sellers are in equilibrium or disequilibrium about price. When pattern confirms what price has alerted us to, we then look to our last method of analysis, time, to confirm the change in trend.

Time

All markets run in cycles, from low to high to low, and each of these cycles reflects the human emotions of fear and greed. Economic cycles, business cycles, stock market cycles, property cycles—are all influenced by human behaviour. Indeed, the basic laws of supply and demand dictate the rise and fall of prices in all markets.

When buying a stock, you do not want demand to accelerate, as this forces prices higher too quickly, making it difficult to purchase at the price you want. In contrast, when you sell, you do want more competition, as the greater the demand from buyers the better your exit price is likely to be. So how do you know when demand will most likely rise or when it will most likely fall? The answer is in understanding cycles.

Using time enables you to identify, with the highest probability, where the market or a stock will likely turn in price. This allows you to be proactive in your trading, as you are using a leading indicator.

The exact timing of a high or low is not something that is consistently predictable, even by the best experts. Rather, the study of cycles allows you to determine the likely direction of a stock or market and when that direction may change, so you can time your entry or exit with relative accuracy. This is the very basis of trading: To time your entry and exit so as to extract a reasonable percentage of available profit from a movement in the price of a stock or market.

Once price, pattern and time align, we can enter a trade with confidence, knowing that there is a high probability of the move continuing in the direction we are predicting.

Let's see the effect of using trend lines and stop losses on the portfolio we created in Chapter 4. I will also point out where trades were supported by price, pattern and time.

Riding the waves

If you remember, we invested $100,000 in nine different stocks on 2 January 2007. Whether you reinvest the dividends you receive from your investments will depend on the goal of your portfolio. If you are already in retirement, you will probably want to receive the dividends as income. However, I recommend reinvesting the dividends where possible, as this will compound your returns. For the purpose of this example, I have assumed that the dividends are required as income and so are taken as cash and banked.

As we trade the portfolio, we will use trend lines to filter which stocks to buy or sell on both a weekly and monthly chart, with the decision to trade made using either timeframe. We will also implement a 15 per cent stop loss: To protect capital after we enter a trade, we will sell if it falls 15 per cent below the buy price, with the exit triggered $0.01 below this level. I will also indicate where price, pattern and time support the decision to enter or exit. Remember, the techniques and strategies I present here are timeless in nature; they are useful not only retrospectively but today and into the future.

When trading the stock market, it is important to remember that you should use all of your knowledge all of the time. While two traders or even 100 traders may use the same rules and trading plan, invariably, each will put their own interpretation and personal bias into their trading, with the potential outcome being very different for each individual. This statement is fundamental to understanding how markets move and why there is always opportunity to profit. The simple logic behind this is that our beliefs, fears and greed influence the decisions we make and, as we know, everyone is different.

Remember, my overall goal with the portfolio is to generate growth and income over the long term by holding between 5 and 12 stocks selected from the top twenty on the ASX. To avoid any bias, the initial portfolio will commence with nine stocks, as all nine meet the selection criteria outlined in Chapter 4 and provided a buying opportunity on 2 January 2007. In addition, all prices have been adjusted to account for any corporate actions that took place during the period we traded the portfolio.

Table 6.1, opposite, again lists the stocks purchased on 2 January 2007.

Table 6.1: Stocks purchased on the ASX on 2 January 2007				
Stock code	Buy price	No. of shares	Amount	Total amount[1]
CBA	$49.12	225	$11,052.00	$11,077.00
CSL	$21.67	511	$11,073.37	$11,098.37
FGL	$5.67	1955	$11,084.85	$11,109.85
MQG	$77.80	142	$11,047.60	$11,072.60
NAB	$38.49	288	$11,085.12	$11,110.12
QBE	$28.07	394	$11,059.58	$11,084.58
SGB	$32.97	336	$11,077.92	$11,102.92
SGP	$7.87	1408	$11,080.96	$11,105.96
WDC	$10.48	1057	$11,077.36	$11,102.36

1. After brokerage costs of $25 or 0.1% per transaction, whichever is greater

Because stocks rise and fall, returns can vary widely from one year to the next. It is, therefore, important that returns are only assessed over multiple years. For this reason, I have managed the portfolio over ten years to take into account the effect of the GFC and the market volatility that followed this period. I have provided the cumulative returns in table format so you can see how the portfolio evolved over the period.

To make it easy to understand how to interpret the tables, I have provided some guidelines below:

- Buy price: The price paid to purchase the stock.
- Total invested: The total amount invested after taking into consideration brokerage (with the cash balance reduced by the brokerage fee).
- Price as at: The closing price of the stock on the last trading day of the year (on or before 31 December using adjusted data).
- Growth %: The capital growth of the stock from the date it was purchased.
- Capital gain/loss: The increase/decrease in value since it was purchased.
- Total value: The total value of the stock in dollar terms at the end of each year.

- Cash balance: This represents all dividends banked during the period and any money received through the sale of stocks.

Results Year 1: 2 January 2007 to 31 December 2007

During the first year, we bought four stocks and sold nine. We sold out of NAB, QBE, Stockland and Macquarie after the stocks triggered an exit on a weekly trend line, while Westfield and St George triggered an exit on a monthly trend line. NAB and Westfield sold at a loss of 2.29 per cent and 4.73 per cent respectively, although Westfield did receive a dividend during the time we held it. The remaining stocks returned a profit as follows: QBE Insurance 7.55 per cent, Stockland 2.72 per cent, Macquarie 11.91 per cent and St George 5.51 per cent, inclusive of dividends.

We also sold Fosters Group after it gapped down through the stop loss by over 3 per cent, resulting in a loss of 15.10 per cent inclusive of a dividend. We managed to buy Woodside following a trend line entry on the monthly chart and Telstra on the weekly chart, although we sold out of Woodside after triggering a trend line exit on the weekly chart for a profit of 5.70 per cent. Another opportunity also came up to purchase Stockland and St George, with both stocks triggering an entry on the weekly chart, although we had to sell Stockland just over three months later following a trend line exit on the weekly chart, resulting in a small profit of 1.86 per cent inclusive of a dividend.

Stock Code	Buy Price	Total Invested	Price#	Growth (%)	Capital Gain/Loss#	Total Value
Table 6.2: Results year 1, 2 January 2007 to 31 December 2007						
CBA	$49.12	$11,052.00	$58.78	19.67%	$2,173.50	$13,225.50
CSL	$21.67	$11,073.37	$36.36	67.79%	$7,506.59	$18,579.96
FGL	$5.67	$11,084.85	Sold			
MQG	$77.80	$11,047.60	Sold			
NAB	$38.49	$11,085.12	Sold			
QBE	$28.07	$11,059.58	Sold			
SGB	$32.97	$11,077.92	Sold			
SGP	$7.87	$11,080.96	Sold			
WDC	$10.48	$11,077.36	Sold			
WPL	$38.55	$13,839.45	Sold			
SGP	$8.30	$13,197.00	Sold			
SGB	$36.60	$13,285.80	$31.59	-13.69%	-$1,818.63	$11,467.17
TLS	$4.56	$13,410.96	$4.69	2.85%	$382.33	$13,793.29

Total value of shares	$57,065.92
Cash balance (bank)	$54,335.22
Total	**$111,401.14**
Less starting amount	$100,000.00
Portfolio profit/(loss)	**$11,401.14**
% Gain	**11.40%**

as at 31/12/2007

Note: Results are cumulative from 2/01/2007 to the end of the period.

Tax and inflation have not been taken into consideration.

During 2007, my analysis of the overall market was that it would peak before declining around 30 per cent or more. While I communicated this at many public events and in publications throughout 2006 and 2007, my advice was ignored, as many believed the market would continue to trade higher on unprecedented euphoria.

Despite the market being at risk of the long-term uptrend failing, as you can see, there were still opportunities to buy good quality companies throughout 2007, although it did require us to be more cautious about the number of trades we placed.

While the return on Macquarie was not that spectacular given that it traded up just over six months, we did protect capital, as only eight weeks after exiting, price fell a further 28 per cent, and in the twelve months following the exit, it fell over 55 per cent in price, as you can see in Figure 6.1, below.

Figure 6.1: Performance of Macquarie Group

While we exited Macquarie after it closed twice below the uptrend line on a weekly chart, as you can see, it also fell below the uptrend line on the monthly chart. The weekly trend line allowed us to exit six weeks earlier and around 12.50 per cent higher at $85.54 than if we had waited for the close below the monthly trend line.

As shown on the chart opposite, I placed a price and time probability box on the stock as my analysis indicated that Macquarie would fall into a low some time between December 2006 and August 2008, with price likely to find support between $38.07 and $57.72.

The application of pattern analysis also indicated that the completion of the uptrend was to occur around $91.44, as shown by the horizontal line on the chart. As you can see, the analysis indicated that the uptrend was coming to an end and the stock would fall in price. This is not too dissimilar to what was occurring with many other top stocks around that time.

At the end of the first year, the portfolio achieved a profit of $11,401.14 or a gain of 11.40 per cent, which included income from dividends of $2,941.44.

Results Year 2: 2 January 2008 to 31 December 2008

The market peaked in November 2007 and fell heavily for five months before turning to trade up, although all indications were that the market was still bearish and likely to fall further. And from May 2008 until March 2009, the market continued its decline, catching out many investors with the severity of the fall.

As market sentiment was bearish, we only bought Fosters Group, following a trend line entry on the monthly chart, and we sold CBA, CSL, St George and Telstra after triggering a trend line exit on the monthly chart. Both CBA and CSL returned a profit of 6.21 per cent and 66.22 per cent respectively, inclusive of dividends, while St George and Telstra suffered a loss of 11.53 per cent and 0.37 per cent respectively, including dividends.

Overall, the portfolio only managed a two-year profit of 8.94 per cent, although considering this was the start of the GFC, it is pretty impressive when you consider the market fell 35 per cent, or 1,985 points, from 2 January 2007 (5,644 points) to 31 December 2008 (3,659 points).

This result highlights why it is essential not only to protect capital by implementing a stop loss but also to have an exit strategy to protect profits.

Table 6.3: Results year 2, 2 January 2008 to 31 December 2008

Stock Code	Buy Price	Total Invested	Price#	Growth (%)	Capital Gain/Loss#	Total Value
CBA	$49.12	$11,052.00	Sold			
CSL	$21.67	$11,073.37	Sold			
SGB	$36.60	$13,285.80	Sold			
TLS	$4.56	$13,410.96	Sold			
FGL	$4.50	$11,479.50	$4.48	-0.44%	-$51.02	$11,428.48

Total value of shares	$11,428.48
Cash balance (bank)	$97,508.70
Total	**$108,937.18**
Less starting amount	$100,000.00
Portfolio profit/(loss)	**$8,937.18**
% Gain	**8.94%**

as at 31/12/2008

Note: Results are cumulative from 2/01/2007 to the end of the period.

Tax and inflation have not been taken into consideration.

As shown in Figure 6.2, opposite, the monthly trend line triggered an exit on CSL at $34.88, producing a very healthy profit of 66.22 per cent, including dividends. This is a good example of why you need to continually apply your rules regardless of the market conditions, as CSL continued to rise to a high in May 2008 despite the market falling heavily.

Figure 6.2: Performance of CSL

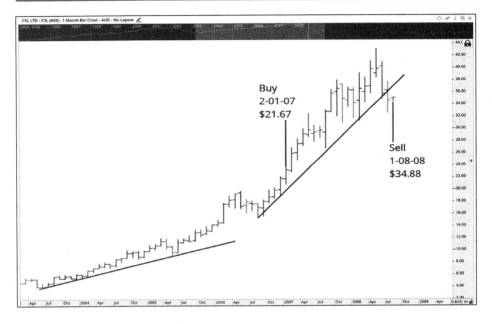

Results Year 3: 2 January 2009 to 31 December 2009

The third year was a little more active, as we bought ten stocks including CSL, BHP, RIO, Woodside, Stockland, CBA, ANZ, NAB, Westfield and Macquarie. All stocks triggered an entry on the weekly trend line, with the exception of ANZ and Macquarie, which triggered an entry on the monthly trend line. We also sold eight stocks, as all stocks except CSL and BHP triggered a trend line exit on the weekly chart. Woodside, Stockland, NAB, Westfield and Macquarie returned a profit of 36.49 per cent, 49.87 per cent, 38.06 per cent, 20.75 per cent and 55.18 per cent respectively, while Fosters was sold at a small loss of 0.38 per cent, inclusive of dividends. CSL and BHP also sold at a loss of 14.55 per cent and 13.26 per cent, inclusive of dividends, after triggering the 15 per cent stop loss.

Table 6.4: Results year 3, 2 January 2009 to 31 December 2009

Stock Code	Buy Price	Total Invested	Price#	Growth (%)	Capital Gain/Loss#	Total Value
FGL	$4.50	$11,479.50	Sold			
CSL	$35.65	$13,012.25	Sold			
BHP	$30.38	$13,088.40	Sold			
RIO	$39.44	$13,054.64	$74.89	89.88%	$11,733.95	$24,788.59
WPL	$34.88	$12,626.56	Sold			
SGP	$2.74	$12,532.76	Sold			
CBA	$33.32	$12,528.32	$54.55	63.72%	$7,982.48	$20,510.80
ANZ	$15.77	$13,026.02	$22.88	45.09%	$5,872.86	$18,898.88
NAB	$20.38	$13,022.82	Sold			
WDC	$5.39	$13,739.11	Sold			
MQG	$30.49	$13,293.64	Sold			

Total value of shares	$64,198.27
Cash balance (bank)	$93,949.41
Total	**$158,147.68**
Less starting amount	$100,000.00
Portfolio profit/(loss)	**$58,147.68**
% Gain	**58.15%**

as at 31/12/2009

Note: Results are cumulative from 2/01/2007 to the end of the period.

Tax and inflation have not been taken into consideration.

This year, the market transitioned from being overly bearish during the GFC to finding support and rising once again, with the market producing more opportunities to buy than we could accommodate given that the cash balance in the bank account was fully invested when opportunities arose. At the end of the third year, the investment value had increased to 58.15 per cent, or an average annual return of 19.40 per cent.

As you can see in Figure 6.3, below, NAB triggered an entry relatively early, as the new uptrend unfolded after closing twice above the downtrend line. The stock also triggered an exit within 13 per cent of the high that occurred in October 2009 to deliver a solid profit, even though the market was still volatile and punishing stocks, with many falling away in price.

Figure 6.3: Performance of NAB

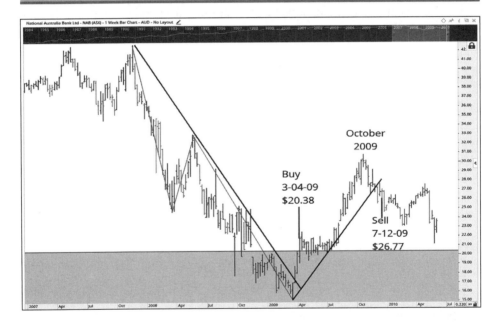

At the time, the analyses of price, pattern and time on NAB were aligned to support the decision to enter the stock. As shown on the chart above, the price and time probability box indicated that NAB was due to fall into a major low, given that the stock had been in a decline for well over a year, and, as such, it was likely once the low was confirmed that direction would change. The decline also confirmed the final phase of a pattern, both in form and in the degree of the fall, which supported the view that the low in 2009 would likely be the end of the decline.

Results Year 4: 4 January 2010 to 31 December 2010

Again, this year, we were more active, buying six stocks, including CSL and Suncorp after they triggered a trend line entry on the monthly chart and NAB, Westfield, Brambles, and QBE after they triggered a trend line entry on the weekly chart. We sold four stocks, with three of the stocks producing a profit, including dividends, as follows: RIO 72.18 per cent and CBA 64.18 per cent following a trend line exit on the weekly chart, and ANZ 50.76 per cent after triggering a trend line exit on the monthly chart.

While NAB triggered a signal to buy during the year, the stock performed poorly and fell heavily in price to trigger the initial stop, resulting in a loss of 15.28 per cent. This emphasizes the point that trend lines are not always going to provide a profitable result and using a stop loss helps to protect capital.

As a result of the volatility, the portfolio lost ground, achieving a four-year return of 56.61 per cent. This would, however, be considered a good result given that the overall market closed up less than 1 per cent for the year.

Stock Code	Buy Price	Total Invested	Price#	Growth (%)	Capital Gain/Loss#/	Total Value
RIO	$39.44	$13,054.64	Sold			
CBA	$33.32	$12,528.32	Sold			
ANZ	$15.77	$13,026.02	Sold			
CSL	$35.16	$18,599.64	$36.29	3.21%	$597.77	$19,197.41
NAB	$25.48	$18,753.28	Sold			
WDC	$6.27	$18,872.70	$6.05	-3.51%	-$662.20	$18,216.55
BXB	$5.43	$18,011.31	$6.62	21.92%	$3,947.23	$21,965.16
QBE	$17.45	$18,322.50	$17.66	1.20%	$220.50	$18,560.66
SUN	$8.71	$18,351.97	$8.17	-6.20%	-$1,137.78	$17,222.36

Table 6.5: Results year 4, 4 January 2010 to 31 December 2010

Total value of shares	$95,162.14
Cash balance (bank)	$61,445.01
Total	**$156,607.15**
Less starting amount	$100,000.00
Portfolio profit/(loss)	**$56,607.15**
% Gain	**56.61%**

as at 31/12/2010

Note: Results are cumulative from 2/01/2007 to the end of the period.

Tax and inflation have not been taken into consideration.

This year, the market was quite volatile. This can cause immense frustration for traders, as stocks can present false triggers, resulting in losses from being stopped out of trades. These false triggers affect a trader's psychology and belief in themselves, and in their trading plan. It can also cause traders to become inpatient, which results in rash, emotional decisions in order to make up for losses.

Therefore, it is important to remember that while trading is a science, it is also an art form, and, at times, even the best analysis is not enough, simply because the market is subject to human emotions. This is the reason why it is vitally important to not only manage your portfolio, during periods of volatility or when the market is falling, but also your psychology. Always remember, there are times when you should trade and times when you should stay out the market, which is often dictated by the market itself. There are also times when a person is not psychologically in the right frame of mind to trade, and it is more dangerous to trade during these times than when the market is volatile.

If you want to continue achieving profitable returns, you want to be in the market when you (and the market) are in the best position to profit, and you want to exit when it is not conducive for you to profit, as this will have a detrimental effect on the portfolio. Doing so will enable the compounding effect on your money to continue working.

Figure 6.4, opposite, is a monthly chart showing the strong rise on CBA following the trend line entry at $33.32, with a trend line exit triggered at $52.81. Both the entry and exit were triggered on the weekly chart. The month prior to the stock triggering an entry, CBA presented a strong bullish pattern to support the decision to enter the trade and a pattern indicating where the stock was likely to peak, supporting the decision to exit.

Price and time aligned to alert us that the stock would fall away into a low. While the low occurred just prior to the expected timeframe, as indicated by the price and time probability box, it did fall to the predicted price level. Sometimes you will see price and time come in just short of or just after a target zone due to a variety of factors. This analysis highlights that we must be flexible in our thinking and use all of our knowledge to assess what will most likely unfold to ensure we protect capital.

Figure 6.4: Performance of CBA

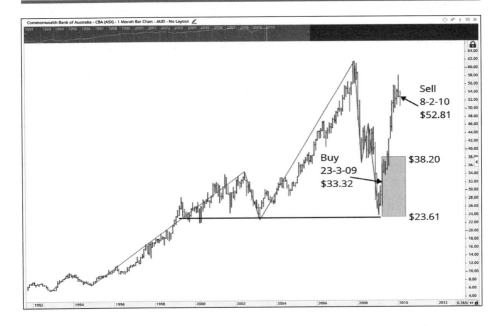

Results Year 5: 3 January 2011 to 31 December 2011

The market continued to be volatile throughout 2011, resulting in the portfolio losing ground once again to achieve a five-year return on our initial investment of 53.33 per cent. Occasionally, you will experience long-term volatility in the stock market, although when you do, it is wise to be patient and stick to your plan. Conditions will change and you need to be ready for when this occurs. All too often, people lose patience and start chasing returns in other markets, only to find that they miss great opportunities when favourable conditions return.

During the year, we bought seven stocks, including Macquarie, NAB, Telstra and ANZ after they triggered a trend line entry on the monthly chart, and Westfield and Suncorp following a trend line entry on the weekly chart. We exited NAB after it triggered an exit on the monthly trend line, delivering a profit of 3 per cent, inclusive of a dividend, although it did provide another trend line entry on the weekly chart later in the year.

We also sold CSL, Brambles, QBE and Suncorp after they triggered a trend line exit on the weekly chart and Macquarie after it triggered the initial stop to incur a loss of 15.27 per cent. While Brambles and CSL achieved a profit, including dividends, of 27.03 per cent and 3.82 per cent respectively, we sold Suncorp and QBE for a loss of 9.56 per cent and 3.76 per cent respectively, inclusive of dividends. Westfield also triggered an exit after the stock fell to trade below the lowest low immediately prior to it trading above the trend line. (A stock that is in an uptrend would continually achieve higher lows or troughs, but when it makes a lower low, it suggests that the downtrend is continuing, therefore, you need to exit to protect capital. We discuss this concept in more detail in Chapter 8.)

While you may be thinking it would have been better to hold Suncorp (which triggered an entry in late 2010) and NAB rather than pay brokerage to exit and re-enter the stock, it is important to remember that at the time the exit is triggered, it is unknown how far the stock is likely to fall, therefore, you are better off exiting to protect capital.

Stock Code	Buy Price	Total Invested	Price#	Growth (%)	Capital Gain/Loss#	Total Value
CSL	$35.16	$18,599.64	Sold			
WDC	$6.27	$18,872.70	Sold			
BXB	$5.43	$18,011.31	Sold			
QBE	$17.45	$18,322.50	Sold			
SUN	$8.71	$18,351.97	Sold			
MQG	$40.07	$18,752.76	Sold			
NAB	$23.25	$18,762.75	Sold			
TLS	$3.02	$18,615.28	$3.33	10.26%	$1,910.84	$20,532.78
NAB	$23.33	$18,454.03	$22.22	-4.76%	-$878.01	$17,576.02
SUN	$8.28	$18,646.56	$7.95	-3.99%	-$743.16	$17,911.35
ANZ	$21.26	$18,538.72	$20.53	-3.43%	-$636.56	$17,922.69
WDC	$5.28	$18,416.64	$4.93	-6.63%	-$1,220.80	$17,195.84

Table 6.6: Results year 5, 3 January 2011 to 31 December 2011

Total value of shares	$91,138.68
Cash balance (bank)	$62,188.85
Total	**$153,327.53**
Less starting amount	$100,000.00
Portfolio profit/(loss)	**$53,327.53**
% Gain	**53.33%**

as at 31/12/2011

Note: Results are cumulative from 2/01/2007 to the end of the period.

Tax and inflation have not been taken into consideration.

Westfield was an interesting trade and a perfect example of how you can apply all of your analysis and have probability in your favour, only to find the stock does not unfold as expected.

In Figure 6.5, below, Westfield rose from $4.33 in March 2009 to a high of $7.15 in October 2009 before falling away to a low of $5.74 in February 2010. The stock found support at 50 per cent of the distance it rose between March and October 2009, which is a sign of strength. Eight weeks after the low in February 2010, price traded up through the weekly downtrend line, while at the same time it broke above a pattern to trigger an entry at $6.27. Therefore, we have price and pattern indicating that a new uptrend is potentially unfolding.

Figure 6.5: Performance of Westfield

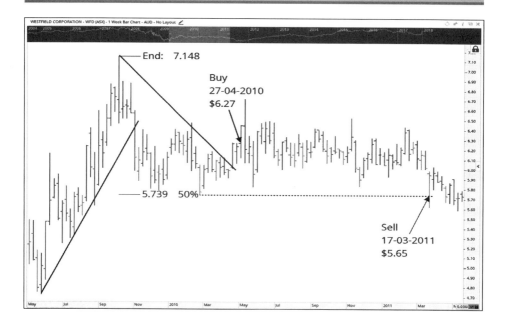

Yet, as you can see on the chart above, price traded sideways for quite some time before falling below the low in February 2010 to continue the prior downtrend, triggering an exit at $5.65 and a small loss of 0.02 per cent due to the fact we received two dividends while holding the stock. Contrary to what you might think, I would consider this a successful trade; we followed our rules and protected capital. This is a very important concept to grasp because you will, no doubt, have losing trades; it is how you manage these trades that will determine your overall profitability.

Results Year 6: 3 January 2012 to 31 December 2012

This year the portfolio performed strongly, rising 37.67 per cent on the previous year and returning an average annual return of 15.17 per cent. We bought five stocks and sold two, with RIO triggering a weekly trend line entry at $69.28 before it fell heavily to trigger the 15 per cent stop loss. As we received a dividend during the time we held RIO, it reduced the overall loss to 14.45 per cent. Once again, there were additional opportunities to buy stocks in the top twenty during the year, however, we were unable to take advantage of these given that the cash balance in the bank account was fully invested, which is a common occurrence when the market is rising.

In addition to RIO, we also bought CBA, Macquarie, Woolworths and Wesfarmers, which all triggered a trend line entry on the monthly chart. We also sold Telstra after triggering a trend line exit on the weekly chart at a profit of 18.91 per cent, including dividends, with the performance shown in Figure 6.6 on page 103.

Table 6.7: Results year 6, 3 January 2012 to 31 December 2012

Stock Code	Buy Price	Total Invested	Price#	Growth (%)	Capital Gain/Loss#	Total Value
TLS	$3.02	$18,615.28	Sold			
NAB	$23.33	$18,454.03	$23.78	1.93%	$355.95	$18,809.98
SUN	$8.28	$18,646.56	$9.81	18.48%	$3,445.56	$22,101.93
ANZ	$21.26	$18,538.72	$25.05	17.83%	$3,304.88	$21,868.65
WDC	$5.28	$18,416.64	$6.66	26.14%	$4,813.44	$23,230.08
RIO	$69.28	$18,705.60	Sold			
CBA	$50.43	$18,709.53	$61.84	22.63%	$4,233.11	$22,942.64
MQG	$26.19	$18,725.85	$34.90	33.26%	$6,227.65	$24,953.50
WOW	$26.41	$19,358.53	$29.33	11.06%	$2,140.36	$21,498.89
WES	$32.46	$20,027.82	$36.79	13.34%	$2,671.61	$22,699.43

Total value of shares	$178,105.10
Cash balance (bank)	$12,895.29
Total	**$191,000.39**
Less starting amount	$100,000.00
Portfolio profit/(loss)	**$91,000.39**
% Gain	**91.00%**

\# as at 31/12/2012

Note: Results are cumulative from 2/01/2007 to the end of the period.

Tax and inflation have not been taken into consideration.

This year's result was even more spectacular given that, once again, we had to endure continued volatility. Market sentiment was still not high and world markets were on edge. Any bad news released resulted in both stocks and the market being punished. During the year, the market rose around 10 per cent before falling nearly 11 per cent to eventually rise just under 14 per cent.

On the monthly chart of Telstra, Figure 6.6, below, pattern analysis allowed us to confirm the low of $2.55 in November 2010. There is also a second slightly higher low some four months later in March 2011 at $2.57. Once price rose up through the downtrend line, it confirmed that the downtrend was most likely over and we entered the trade at $3.02 in June 2011. The stock continued to trade up before finding resistance at around the $3.30 to $3.40 price level. Given the volatility in the market at the time, the decision was made to exit using the weekly trend line (not shown) in March 2012 at $3.32.

While we made a profit, in hindsight, using the monthly trend line to exit would have achieved a much higher profit. However, we cannot trade in hindsight. Given the economic uncertainty and unrest at the time, the best outcome was to take the lower risk decision based on what the analysis was telling us at the time.

Figure 6.6: Performance of Telstra

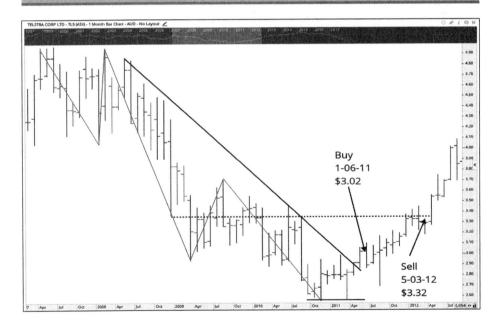

Results Year 7: 2 January 2013 to 31 December 2013

This year proved uneventful in terms of buying opportunities, although we sold three stocks in profit, including dividends, after they triggered a trend line exit on the weekly chart as follows: ANZ 42.85 per cent, Westfield 44.31 per cent and Suncorp 57.38 per cent. Figure 6.7, on page 106, shows the performance of Suncorp.

As you can see, the portfolio performed exceptionally well, rising by 51.36 per cent on the previous year. After seven years, it increased the original investment by 142.36 per cent, or an average annual return of 20.34 per cent.

Because we limited ourselves to only selecting stocks in the top twenty, the cash balance was continually growing while we waited for opportunities to arise. Obviously, if we had considered stocks out to the top fifty, we could potentially have compounded our returns further by purchasing other stocks that were rising in value.

Stock Code	Buy Price	Total Invested	Price[#]	Growth (%)	Capital Gain/Loss[#]	Total Value
Table 6.8: Results year 7, 2 January 2013 to 31 December 2013						
NAB	$23.33	$18,454.03	$33.13	42.01%	$7,751.80	$26,205.83
ANZ	$21.26	$18,538.72	Sold			
WDC	$5.28	$18,416.64	Sold			
SUN	$8.28	$18,646.56	Sold			
CBA	$50.43	$18,709.53	$77.38	53.44%	$9,998.45	$28,707.98
MQG	$26.19	$18,725.85	$54.97	109.89%	$20,577.70	$39,303.55
WOW	$26.41	$19,358.53	$33.85	28.17%	$5,453.52	$24,812.05
WES	$32.46	$20,027.82	$43.92	35.30%	$7,070.82	$27,098.64

Total value of shares	$146,128.05
Cash balance (bank)	$96,232.92
Total	**$242,360.97**
Less starting amount	$100,000.00
Portfolio profit/(loss)	**$142,360.97**
% Gain	**142.36%**

as at 31/12/2013

Note: Results are cumulative from 2/01/2007 to the end of the period.

Tax and inflation have not been taken into consideration.

As I have said before, when trading, it is important to always apply all of your knowledge. As you can see on the chart, Figure 6.7, overleaf, Suncorp was trading above the downtrend line for eight weeks prior to the week we entered the trade. The reason for this is that there was strong price resistance around $8.00, so even though the trend line rules triggered an entry to buy, we only purchased the stock once price closed well above this level, which occurred the week commencing 28 October 2011.

After entering the trade, price moved down and sideways for thirty-two weeks into a yearly low of $7.07 in June 2012. At no time was the 15 per cent stop loss triggered, although it did get very close. As you can see, the stock traded up strongly from the low over the next two years with the trend line exit triggered on the weekly chart in December 2013.

Figure 6.7: Performance of Suncorp

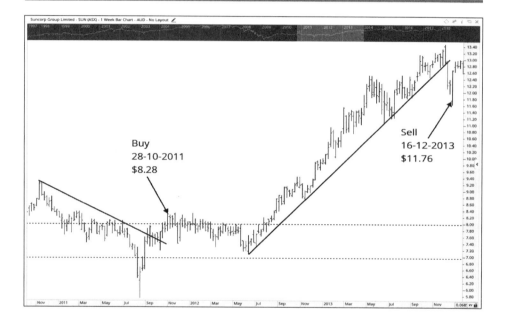

Before moving on, I want to mention an interesting point about what unfolded in 2013. There was much speculation that the US market was likely to fall off a "fiscal cliff", which could have potentially had a flow on effect on the Australian market. However, despite all the speculation, the Dow Jones Index rose over 26 per cent during 2013, while our market rose around 15 per cent, which was the largest move up since the strong rise out of the GFC low in 2009.

Why is this important? Typically, published information is already factored into the price of a market and, therefore, I generally think the opposite of what is being communicated in the news. Remember how we discussed the significance of understanding market moods in Chapter 4? Analysing the movements of the market enables you to be successful, as you aren't subjected to the herd mentality that is so prevalent today.

Results Year 8: 2 January 2014 to 31 December 2014

This year was another strong year, with the portfolio rising 25.98 per cent on the previous year to achieve a gain on the original investment of 168.34 per cent.

We bought four stocks, including AMP, Westfield, CBA and CSL after they triggered a trend line entry on the weekly chart, and we sold six stocks. All stocks were sold at a profit with the following increases, including dividends: NAB 60.13 per cent, Woolworths 41.19 per cent, Wesfarmers 37.29 per cent and Macquarie 139.78 per cent. These all triggered a trend line exit on the monthly chart, while CBA triggered a trend line exit on the weekly chart, achieving a return of 59.45 per cent. CBA also triggered another entry and exit later in the year on a weekly trend line for a profit of 6.37 per cent. This year also saw Westfield relist on the stock exchange using the ASX code WFD.

Table 6.9: Results year 8, 2 January 2014 to 31 December 2014

Stock Code	Buy Price	Total Invested	Price#	Growth (%)	Capital Gain/Loss#	Total Value
NAB	$23.33	$18,454.03	Sold			
CBA	$50.43	$18,709.53	Sold			
MQG	$26.41	$18,725.85	Sold			
WOW	$26.41	$19,358.53	Sold			
WES	$32.46	$20,027.82	Sold			
AMP	$4.97	$29,109.29	$5.50	10.66%	$3,104.21	$32,219.00
WFD	$6.50	$29,022.50	$9.02	38.77%	$11,251.80	$40,274.30
CBA	$76.14	$29,313.90	Sold			
CSL	$72.87	$30,824.01	$86.68	18.95%	$5,841.63	$36,665.64

Total value of shares	$109,158.94
Cash balance (bank)	$159,178.03
Total	**$268,336.97**
Less starting amount	$100,000.00
Portfolio profit/(loss)	**$168,336.97**
% Gain	**168.34%**

as at 31/12/2014

Note: Results are cumulative from 2/01/2007 to the end of the period.

Tax and inflation have not been taken into consideration.

The monthly chart of Woolworths, Figure 6.8, opposite, shows how the stock rose strongly for twenty-nine months. This is not surprising, as the length of an uptrend will generally last anywhere up to three years or more on big blue chip stocks.

Figure 6.8: Performance of Woolworths

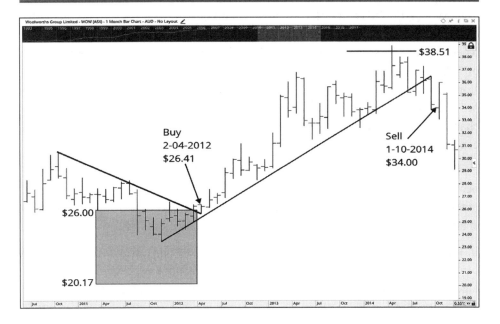

The trigger to buy was supported by the fact that Woolworths had fallen into a four-year low, as shown by the price and time probability box, which indicated that we were expecting the low to occur somewhere between $20.17 and $26. The eventual low occurred in November 2011 at $23.49, with the monthly bar creating a bullish pattern. This means we now had price, pattern and time confirming a likely change in trend. Four months later, price moved above the monthly downtrend line to trigger an entry at $26.41.

Woolworths continued to trade up nicely, reaching a high of $38.92 in April 2014, which was very close to previous price resistance at $38.51. At the time, my analysis also indicated that the stock was due to move into a longer-term low in the next eighteen months. Therefore, once price fell below the monthly uptrend line, we exited the stock.

Results Year 9: 2 January 2015 to 31 December 2015

Once again, we had an active year, buying six stocks, including NAB, ANZ, Westpac, QBE, CSL and CBA, with NAB and QBE triggering a trend line entry on the monthly chart. The remaining stocks triggered a trend line entry on the weekly chart. We sold seven stocks, all of which were in profit with the exception of NAB and ANZ. NAB fell heavily after entering, triggering the 15 per cent stop loss, although we did receive a dividend reducing the overall loss to 12.27 per cent. ANZ also performed poorly following a trend line entry on the weekly chart, with a trend line exit triggered on the monthly chart for a loss of 4.62 per cent, including dividends.

Of the stocks that made a profit, AMP returned 30.83 per cent, Westfield 60.82 per cent, CSL 25.17 per cent, Westpac 11.09 per cent and QBE 7.58 per cent, inclusive of dividends, after all stocks triggered a trend line exit on the weekly chart. Figure 6.9, on page 112, shows the performance of QBE.

In the nine years since 2 January 2007, the portfolio has grown by 187.15 per cent, with an increase in value of 18.81 per cent on the previous year. Since inception, it has produced an average annual return of 20.79 per cent.

Stock Code	Buy Price	Total Invested	Price#	Growth (%)	Capital Gain/Loss#	Total Value
Table 6.10: Results year 9, 2 January 2015 to 31 December 2015						
AMP	$4.97	$29,109.29	Sold			
WFD	$6.50	$29,022.50	Sold			
CSL	$72.87	$30,824.01	Sold			
NAB	$33.89	$32,873.30	Sold			
WBC	$34.40	$32,886.40	Sold			
ANZ	$34.75	$33,672.75	Sold			
QBE	$12.70	$34,518.60	Sold			
CSL	$93.60	$33,602.40	$105.31	12.51%	$4,203.89	$37,806.29
CBA	$80.25	$33,865.50	$85.53	6.58%	$2,228.16	$36,179.19

Total value of shares	$73,985.48
Cash balance (bank)	$213,165.97
Total	**$287,151.45**
Less starting amount	$100,000.00
Portfolio profit/(loss)	**$187,151.45**
% Gain	**187.15%**

\# as at 31/12/2015

Note: Results are cumulative from 2/01/2007 to the end of the period.

Tax and inflation have not been taken into consideration.

While we only held QBE for just over three months, we were able to achieve a return of 7.58 per cent, including dividends, which is acceptable. The entry on this trade was a little more unusual than others given that in late December 2013 the stock fell to just above a heavy support level at $9.11. It then traded up, sideways and down into January 2015 to within $0.07 of the December 2013 low, which is known as a "double bottom" pattern. The stock also had strong support and looked to have completed a yearly low, so, once again, we had price, pattern and time indicating a change in trend was highly likely. That said, QBE is known for its volatility, so we used the monthly chart to confirm the entry, as it is more conservative.

While Figure 6.9, below, is a weekly chart, I have drawn a downtrend line on the chart to demonstrate the one drawn on the monthly chart, which triggered an entry at $12.70 in March 2015. Given the stock's volatility, we used the weekly chart to determine the trend line exit so as to protect profits.

Figure 6.9: Performance of QBE Insurance

Results Year 10: 4 January 2016 to 31 December 2016

This year also turned out to be very active, as we bought nine stocks. Stockland, NAB, ANZ, Suncorp, Woolworths, Woodside and Westpac all triggered a trend line entry on the monthly chart, while BHP and CBA triggered a trend line entry on the weekly chart. We also sold three stocks. CSL and Stockland triggered a trend line exit on the weekly chart and returned a profit of 12.25 per cent and 12.38 per cent respectively, including dividends. CBA achieved a minor loss of 1.13 per cent after also triggering a trend line exit on the weekly chart. Figure 6.10, on page 115, shows the performance of Stockland.

Once again, the portfolio continued to rise strongly, by another 38.67 per cent on the previous year, to achieve a rolling return since inception of 225.82 per cent, or an average annual return of 22.58 per cent. Not bad considering the market was still trading well below the previous all-time high that occurred in 2007.

Table 6.11: Results year 10, 4 January 2016 to 31 December 2016

Stock Code	Buy Price	Total Invested	Price#	Growth (%)	Capital Gain/Loss#	Total Value
CSL	$93.60	$33,602.40	Sold			
CBA	$80.25	$33,865.50	Sold			
SGP	$4.15	$34,096.40	Sold			
BHP	$19.86	$34,179.06	$25.06	26.18%	$8,949.20	$43,128.26
NAB	$26.72	$34,468.80	$30.67	14.78%	$5,095.50	$39,564.30
ANZ	$25.12	$34,364.16	$30.42	21.10%	$7,250.40	$41,614.56
SUN	$13.44	$35,118.72	$13.52	0.60%	$209.04	$35,341.28
WOW	$23.41	$35,115.00	$24.10	2.95%	$1,035.00	$36,150.00
WPL	$28.57	$35,341.09	$31.16	9.07%	$3,203.83	$38,576.08
WBC	$30.30	$35,784.30	$32.60	7.59%	$2,716.30	$38,533.20
CBA	$76.79	$36,244.88	$82.41	7.32%	$2,652.64	$38,897.52

Total value of shares	$311,805.20
Cash balance (bank)	$14,019.54
Total	**$325,824.74**
Less starting amount	$100,000.00
Portfolio profit/(loss)	**$225,824.74**
% Gain	**225.82%**

as at 31/12/2016

Note: Results are cumulative from 2/01/2007 to the end of the period.

Tax and inflation have not been taken into consideration.

On the weekly chart of Stockland, Figure 6.10, below, you will notice I have marked the lows that occurred in October 2014 and October 2015. Following the October 2015 low, price moved up to trade above a weekly downtrend line (dashed line), triggering a potential entry into the stock. However, while it appeared that the stock had confirmed its yearly low, it was better to wait for further confirmation that the uptrend was intact by using a monthly trend line. This occurred seventeen weeks later at $4.15 in March 2016, which was just under 3 per cent higher than the entry trigger on the weekly chart, validating my reason to wait.

Figure 6.10: Performance of Stockland

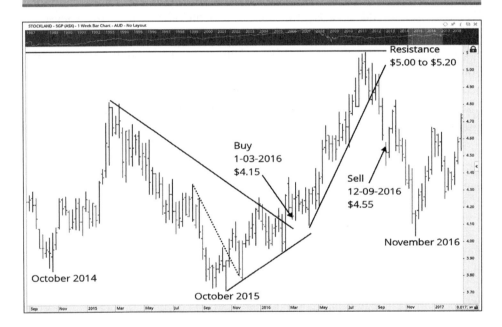

The stock then rose to a high of $5.11 in August 2016, which was in the middle of a price resistance zone of between $5.00 and $5.20. Given that it was reasonable to assume the stock would fall into its yearly low around October 2016, we exited the trade once price fell below the uptrend line on the weekly chart. As you can see, price continued to fall into a low around mid-November 2016.

To sum up

The gain achieved from capital growth and dividends of 225.82 per cent, or an average annual return of 22.58 per cent, over ten years, is impressive considering we are investing for the long term. This equates to an annual compounded rate of return of 12.54 per cent. Obviously, the real return will be lower after factoring in capital gains tax and inflation. But that aside, you can see how it is possible for individuals to achieve very rewarding returns without taking high risks or speculating. By simply using trend lines in combination with a stop loss to protect capital, we beat the compounded rate of return on managed funds, as published by Canstar Research[5], which for the same ten-year period represented only 4.67 per cent.

By now, you should have a good idea how achievable a low-risk, long-term approach to trading the stock market is for the small investor, despite the many cynics who advise otherwise. As I have demonstrated, simply by concentrating your portfolio in the top performing stocks on the ASX, not only can you achieve very profitable returns, but you also have the potential to outperform the institutional returns by 169 per cent, using simple DIY stock market investment strategies.

Chapter 7

The Power of Compounding

"Compound interest is the eighth wonder of the world.
He who understands it, earns it…He who doesn't…pays it."

Albert Einstein

Warren Buffett famously stated that "someone is sitting in the shade today because someone else planted a tree a very long time ago". The true meaning behind this statement is what is referred to as the law of delayed gratification. In other words, by taking action today, you can enjoy prosperity in the future.

Unfortunately, too many people sit on the sidelines waiting for something to happen rather than taking action to make it happen. No doubt you picked up this book because you are looking for security, control and the freedom that financial independence provides. So, I encourage you to take the necessary action that will enable you to achieve your financial goals. The earlier you start, the more you will be able to take advantage of a powerful strategy known as the power of compounding.

Understanding the rule of 72

If you understand the rule of 72, you can compound the success of your investments. Quite simply, if you divide seventy-two by a particular annual return, you will be able to determine how long it will take to double your money. For example, at 7 per cent growth a year, an investment will double in value in a little over ten years. At 14 per cent growth, an investment will double in a little over five years.

In Chapter 6, we had achieved a rolling return of 142.36 per cent by the end of 2013, or an annual compounded return of 13.48 per cent, which means the portfolio doubled in a little over six years, which is pretty impressive.

You can also use the rule of 72 to work out the annual return you require to double your money by dividing seventy-two by the number of years. For example, let's say you want to double your money over eight years; you would simply divide seventy-two by eight to arrive at an annual growth rate of 9 per cent.

The rule of 72 can also be used to calculate the effect of inflation on any money you choose not to invest. For example, if the annual inflation rate is 4 per cent, it will take eighteen years (72/4 = 18 years) before it will be worth half of what it is today.

While the rule of 72 is a simplistic methodology for calculating the time it takes for your initial investment to double or for your money to devalue, it is also important to understand the impact that inflation will have on the growth of your investment over time. Let me explain.

The impact of inflation on your investments

No doubt, you will have heard the common mantra in the financial services industry: Be patient, invest for the long term and diversify your portfolio in order to achieve growth over the longer term. But just what is acceptable growth?

This is where it is important to understand the "required earnings" rate to break even on your investment. Put simply, this is the rate of income or growth you require from your investment each year to keep pace with inflation. Table 7.1, opposite, highlights the earnings rate required at each level of inflation according to the marginal tax rates in Australia.

Table 7.1: Earnings rate required at each level of inflation

Marginal tax rate[1]	Inflation			
	2%	4%	6%	8%
0%	2%	4%	6%	8%
21%	2.53%	5.06%	7.59%	10.13%
34.50%	3.05%	6.11%	9.16%	12.21%
39%	3.28%	6.56%	9.84%	13.11%
47%	3.77%	7.55%	11.32%	15.09%

1. Includes the 2 per cent Medicare levy

Note: Earnings rates are approximate

It is important to ensure that these earning rates are the minimum you are willing to accept on an annual basis under any circumstances.

An after-tax return on your investments that doesn't at least match inflation means you're not saving; you're losing purchasing power. Only if your investment return surpasses inflation can you expect to be truly gaining ground.

According to the Russell Investments/ASX Long-Term Investing Report 2017, the ten-year after-tax return at the top marginal tax rate to 31 December 2016 on Australian shares equates to 3 per cent. The after tax return on the lowest marginal tax for the same period equates to 4.70 per cent. The average inflation rate over the same period was 2.40 per cent, which means your after-tax return needs to be 4.53 per cent on the top marginal tax rate and 3.04 per cent on the lowest marginal tax rate. So it would appear that an investor at the top marginal tax is going backwards.

However, if we consider the returns over twenty years, the after-tax return at the top marginal rate to 31 December 2016 equates to 6.70 per cent, while the after-tax return at the lowest marginal tax rate over the same period equates to 8.70 per cent. So you can see that time is a major factor when it comes to investing in the stock market.

That said, these returns imply that an investor has relied on a passive or buy and hold investment strategy. If we consider a more active investor who times their entry and exits so as to achieve a higher return, you can see that even a 5 per cent variance can make a significant difference over a working lifetime.

Shown in Table 7.2, overleaf, we have two investors who each make regular contributions of $2,000 per year. The first investor achieved a return of 12 per cent per annum, while the second investor achieved a return of 7 per cent per annum. Assuming both continued to contribute $2,000 a year for forty years, you can see what a difference 5 per cent makes over their lifetime.

Table 7.2: 5 per cent can make a real difference		
	Investor 1	**Investor 2**
Amount invested	$80,000	$80,000
Years invested	40	40
Investment value	$1,534,203	$399,273

Now let's investigate why it is important to consider the benefits of compounding your earnings.

Understanding the power of compounding

If you remember in Chapter 2, I discussed the three laws of wealth creation:

1. Spend less than you earn;
2. Invest your surplus wisely (at least 10 per cent of your income); and
3. Leave it alone so it can grow.

While implementing all three rules is important to achieving financial independence, it is the third rule that has the most profound effect on your investments. Let me explain.

Let's assume you have graduated from university and you decide, after getting your first job at twenty-one, to start saving 10 per cent of your income of $65,000. After tax, your take-home pay would be approximately $4,361 per month[1]. Therefore, you would be saving around $436 per month. Your best friend is also working but he decides he would prefer to spend his salary on short-term gratification, as he believes he can start saving later in life.

Now, let's assume you each have $5,000 in the bank, what do you think would be the outcome in ten years' time if the growth rate is 3 per cent per annum?

As shown in Figure 7.1, opposite, the compounding effect is only marginal in the early years, rising from $150 in the first year to $9,379 in Year 10.

---

1. Based on FY 17-18 tax rates

Figure 7.1: Compounded return over 10 years with a savings plan

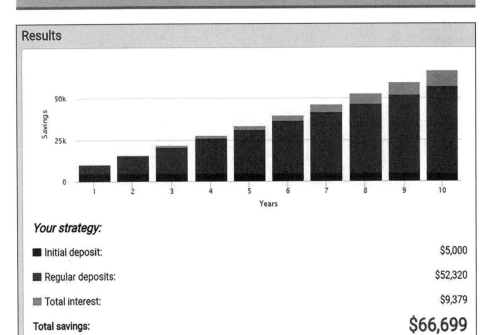

Results

Your strategy:

■ Initial deposit:	$5,000
■ Regular deposits:	$52,320
▨ Total interest:	$9,379
Total savings:	**$66,699**

Source: moneysmart.gov.au

The reason for this is the fact you earn interest on interest as your investments grow. This, therefore, compounds the growth of your investments. And because you have invested your savings on a monthly basis, you have more money working for you. Therefore, your investment has compounded at a much faster rate, which explains why it is so important to leave your investments alone so they can grow. As you can see, at the end of ten years, you would have accumulated $66,699 in wealth.

In comparison, your friend has only accumulated $6,720 in wealth, as shown in Figure 7.2, overleaf. And at a growth rate of 3 per cent, it would take around twenty-four years for the investment to double in value, which is not that exciting.

Figure 7.2: Compounded return over 10 years with no savings plan

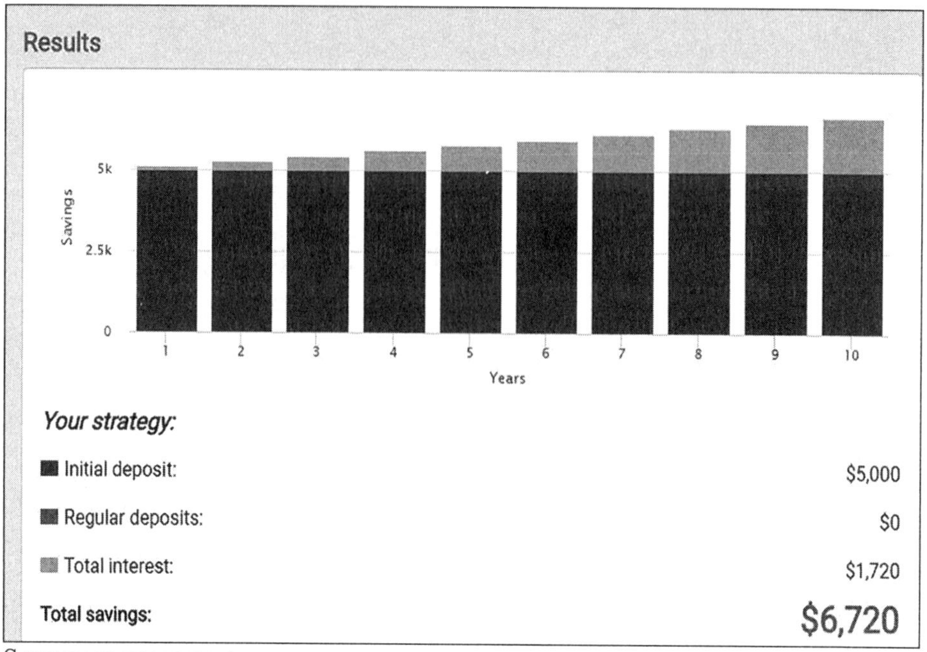

Source: moneysmart.gov.au

So, let's consider how the power of compounding would have affected the portfolios we traded in Chapter 6 if we invested 10 per cent of our income on an annual basis.

Invest at least 10 per cent of your income on an annual basis

Let's assume we have a married couple earning a combined household income of $120,000, with the husband earning $80,000 and the wife working part-time, earning $40,000. Their take-home pay after tax is approximately $94,301.[2] Investing 10 per cent per annum means they would invest around $9,430. So, let's see what the outcome would be if they took advantage of the power of compounding.

As shown in Table 7.3, opposite, you can see we invested an additional $84,870 by depositing $9,430 at the end of the first year of operating the portfolio and every year thereafter. As a consequence, the portfolio grew by an additional $54,830 by the end of 2016 at a compounded annual growth rate of 12.32 per

2. Based on FY 07/08 tax rates, as this is when we would have commenced making additional contributions to the portfolio.

cent[3] in comparison to the portfolio with no additional contributions[4]. Imagine if we continued to invest 10 per cent each year for another ten years.

Table 7.3: Compounded growth over 10 years

	10% contribution p.a.	Nil contributions
Starting Balance	$100,000	$100,000
Contributions	$84,870	Nil
Total Capital	$184,870	$100,000
Growth	$280,720	$225,890
Closing Balance	**$465,590**	**$325,890**

As you can see in Table 7.4, below, if you continued to contribute 10 per cent each year (assuming no growth in your income, change to the rate of return or income tax rates) for another ten years, the portfolio would have grown to over $1.64 million, which is over $414,000 more than if you had simply continued to reinvest your earnings.

Table 7.4: Compounded growth over 20 years

	10% contribution p.a.	Nil contributions
Starting Balance	$100,000	$100,000
Contributions	$179,170	Nil
Total Capital	$279,170	$100,000
Growth	$1,376,799	$962,040
Closing Balance	**$1,655,969**	**$1,062,040**

---

3. The compounded annual rate of return on the portfolio with additional contributions.

4. Using the compounded annual rate of return of 12.54 per cent we achieved on the portfolio in Chapter 6.

While both portfolios grew exponentially as a result of the effects of compounding, the portfolio in which we invested an additional 10 per cent per annum compounded at a much faster rate because we had more money working for us. Obviously, if we had chosen to invest on a monthly basis rather than at the end of each year, the returns would have potentially compounded even further. Either way, the end result is that by compounding your investments, you will achieve your financial goals much sooner.

No doubt you can now appreciate the power of compounding and the three key factors attributable to this technique:

- Rate of return: The higher the return the better, as it will speed up the compounding effect.

- Contributions: The bigger the contribution the better, because you will have more money working for you to compound returns.

- Time: The longer in time you allow your investments to compound the better, because you will be compounding your earnings (from interest, dividends and capital gains).

Capital gains tax

The gain achieved from capital growth and dividends of 225.82 per cent or an average annual return of 22.58 per cent over ten years is impressive considering we are investing for the long term. This equates to an annual compounded rate of return of 12.54 per cent.

Obviously, the real return will be lower after factoring in capital gains tax and inflation. Some may argue that because you have to pay capital gains tax on the shares you sold, you would have done better simply buying and holding. But this is a false assumption—a myth that tends to hinder an investor's ability to generate wealth. While we touched on this myth in Chapter 1, it is important to reiterate the point again.

Imagine you bought $10,000 in shares in one stock and, over a period of three years, you doubled your investment to $20,000. You then decide to sell because the stock has turned and is falling into a downtrend. If you sold, you would be required to pay capital gains tax, but you would only pay this on 50 per cent of the gain of $10,000 because you held the stock for longer than twelve months. Even at the highest marginal tax rate of 47 per cent, you would pay around $2,350, leaving you with $17,650 to reinvest in another stock.

What would be the effect on the portfolio if, instead, you decided to hold the stock and ride out the decline? Remember, most stocks will generally rise for periods of twelve months to five years before falling away for similar periods and, in a decline, stocks will fall as much as 30 per cent or more. This means the stock could potentially fall as much as $6,000 (30 per cent of $20,000), leaving you with far less than if you had exited and paid capital gains tax.

To sum up

A stock that is falling in price not only costs you time in which you could have been compounding your returns, because you have lost the value of your capital, but also opportunity. You cannot take advantage of an asset that is rising if your money is tied up in investments that are falling in value. Consequently, you have also lost valuable time that could have been spent building a profitable portfolio. It is important to value your portfolio return as if you had liquidated your assets today, because the true value is only realised when you sell; up until that point you have made unrealised gains.

During the ten-year period we managed the portfolio, the cash balance (in the bank) fluctuated from around $12,000 to over $213,000. No interest was calculated on these holdings for the period but, in reality, you would have been receiving interest, which would not only have compounded the overall return of the portfolio further but potentially offset some of the capital gains tax you would otherwise pay.

Furthermore, I limited the stocks we could buy in the portfolio to the top twenty on the Australian market. However, we could have invested in other stocks had I included stocks out to the top fifty. Had we invested the surplus cash in other stocks that were rising, we would have potentially compounded even greater returns.

As I have demonstrated throughout this book, some simple yet powerful investment strategies will shield you from losses so that you protect your capital and minimise the risk of losses being compounded. If you take heed of the additional benefits that compounding offers, as outlined in this chapter, I guarantee you will achieve your financial goals much sooner.

Chapter 8

Selling for Profit or Just Selling Out?

"There are two times in a man's life when he should speculate:
When he can't afford it, and when he can"

Mark Twain

Presenting to a group of accountants at CPA Australia[5], I raised the fact that, just as we need to have an exit strategy in business, we also need to have an exit strategy for our investments. When I asked the CPAs attending if they would advise a business owner to sell an unprofitable business, the answer was a resounding yes. I then asked if their advice would be the same for an unprofitable investment and the room went silent.

Remember, one of the key criteria of astute investing is to consider when and how you will take your profits—in other words, you need to consider your exit strategy before you invest. As I have previously stated, many individuals mistakenly believe that not selling a stock that is falling in value means they are not losing. Now let me demonstrate why the opposite is true.

Trading to profit

The fact is, if you want to be consistently profitable, you need to know not only how and why you are entering a trade but also, and more importantly, when and

5. CPAs can only provide advise on investments if they are licensed to do so.

where you will exit. A common statement made by investors is that they only ever achieve a good profit if they pick their entry well. While this statement has some merit, it is only partly true.

You can be right in your analysis less than half the time and still be profitable, as long as the winning trades outperform the losing trades. But what I am proposing is that trading is not just about picking winning trades; rather, trading for profit is about using sound money management rules and good exit strategies.

You have probably heard the saying "You can't go broke taking a profit!" In my opinion, this is a myth, one that is detrimental to your trading and that will set you on a path to financial mediocrity, costing you a lot of money. While we acknowledge we can be right less than half the time and still make money, we can only do this if we allow our profits to run and cut our losses short. I can be right four out of five trades, but my success and profitability will depend on how I handle each trade in regard to my money management and exit rules. Let me explain.

Trading for profit is about using sound money management rules and good exit strategies.

If I have four winning trades that make 20 per cent each and one losing trade that loses 10 per cent, then I am profitable. If I place $1,000 in each trade, I would make $800 and lose $100. Therefore, I would make $700, or around 14 per cent on my capital of $5,000 before costs. However, you need to remember the fact that if I lose 10 per cent, I need to make 11 per cent just to break even again, as we have less capital to re-invest. Now let's look at a slightly different example.

If I decide I am happy making 10 per cent on my profitable trades and I lose 20 per cent on a losing trade then my profitability changes dramatically. Let's say, once again, I place $1,000 in five trades. I would make $400 in total on my winning trades and my losing trade would cost me $200.

As a result, your $400 profit is reduced by half to only $200, and your total return for the five trades is only 4 per cent gross, before costs. Not forgetting the fact that when you lose 20 per cent, you need to make 25 per cent just to break even, so the more you lose, the harder it is to get back on top again. If we allowed the losing trade to continue to fall to a 40 per cent loss then we would be in an unprofitable position on the whole portfolio.

Remember, the longer a stock continues to fall, the greater the effect on your overall profitability. In essence, allowing your losses to run into bigger losses turns a good investment strategy into an average one.

How many times have you decided to take profits on a trade before the stock told you that it wouldn't rise any further, and how many times have you lost 20 to 40 per cent or more on a trade? If you are not consistently profitable, you need to look at your money management rules, which we address later in this chapter, and your exit strategies, rather than spending time trying to pick the next big winner.

If I were to ask you how much time you spend looking for stocks to buy as opposed to the time spent managing your current investments, I can pretty much guess the answer. Every time I ask this question, the overwhelming majority admit they spend most of their time trying to pick the next boom stock. Why is this—because it is more exciting trying to find the next pot of gold? Let me assure you, unless you take care of the current pot so the tree grows and prospers, as Mr Buffett so eloquently stated, it will not survive long enough for you to enjoy it in the future.

So, how do you know when to hold onto stocks and when to sell? The answer will depend on the length of time you want to trade and the type of market you are trading.

It is not uncommon for investors to exit good stocks before there is an indication to do so. However, remember that the market is not 100 per cent black and white. Therefore, you need to allow room for the market to move. We cannot say that a market will turn at an exact point in time or price; we can only indicate with a probability derived from our analysis that this will occur. One of the most important rules I have ever learnt is to trade on confirmation rather than speculation, which means you should never make a decision until the market tells you what it will do.

One of the most important rules in trading is to always trade on confirmation, not speculation.

Stopping the loss

Remember, successfully investing in the stock market is not about how much money you can make; rather it, is about how much you do not lose. In other words, it is about minimising risk not maximising profits. Nonetheless, it has been my experience that many people actually focus on the latter, with little regard for the former. In contrast, the most successful investors I know consistently average a good return on their portfolio by minimising their risk. Not being exposed to heavy losses is, in itself, one of the key principles to successful investing.

In my younger days, I was a ten pin bowler and played in competitions at both regional and state levels. When I first started, I was intrigued by the bowlers who would take a long run up and throw the ball down the lane with such force that you thought the ball would not only knock the pins down but break right through the back wall. I usually referred to these players as strike bowlers because they were unbeatable when they were hot, but when they weren't running so hot, their technique failed to the extent that they couldn't even bowl a second ball to knock out the spares.

Their strategy was all or nothing, which was inconsistent, at best, and high risk. What I came to discover was that the best bowlers were not the strike bowlers but rather those who were able to consistently perform in any condition. These bowlers had a high skill level and a system with which to handle any situation, which meant they won more games and more championships. Given that it was my desire to become a successful bowler, I sought out these consistently good bowlers to model and took them as my mentors. This eventually resulted in me becoming a top class bowler.

The reason I share this story is that this is exactly what happens in trading. Many individuals go for the big hit every time, believing that this is the successful way to trade. And while some are successful in making some great trades, on the whole, they are inconsistent in their results. Over a period of many years, they rarely, if ever, make returns equal to or better than individuals who are consistent in their approach.

If you want to increase your consistency, there are two strategies that you can adopt:

- Take lower risk trades, which will involve staying clear of trading highly leveraged markets until you prove to yourself you can consistently profit from trading stocks directly; and

- Work on setting appropriate stop losses so you are not stopped out too early or, worse, too late.

As we have covered, in simple terms, a stop loss is a price point at which you commit to selling a security. It is used either to preserve capital when a recently entered trade turns against you or to protect the profits of a winning trade. When constructing your trading plan (which we discuss in the next chapter), you need to decide on your exit strategy, as it is usually too late to do this when a stock is falling—simply because your money is on the line, and most investors make emotional rather than rational decisions when it comes to holding or selling a stock at this time. Furthermore, it is often hard to admit, once you take a position on a stock, that you have made a mistake in your analysis, and it is even harder to be objective when losing money.

When calculating a stop loss, you need to use the most recent price available to determine your "buy price". This will be the closing price for the previous day or week. It is imperative that you calculate your stop loss before you buy so that you can work out the risk you are willing to take. After doing so, you may find that you do not want to buy the stock if the risk is too high.

When it comes to actually setting the stop loss, there are a number of different strategies you should consider.

Setting a stop loss

Setting stop losses on stocks can be challenging. You need to be close enough to your buy price to ensure you do not lose more than 2 per cent of your total capital, yet far enough away that the stock has room to move, in case it falls for a short period of time after you buy into it. Individuals frequently set stop losses far too tight and end up losing money, only to find that the stock rises again after they are stopped out.

When setting a stop loss on blue chip stocks, there are a couple of options. Set as a percentage of the buy price, a stop loss is usually 10 to 15 per cent below your buy price (depending on the volatility of the stock), as this allows for minor fluctuations in price as the stock settles into the trend. Setting a stop loss too tight (say 5 per cent below your buy price) leaves very little room for the stock to move and will decrease your probability of a winning trade. Alternatively, you can set the stop loss at a price point where you know with high probability that you may be wrong in your analysis.

I recommend calculating both stop losses and then using the one that gives you the least amount of loss.

Percentage-based stop loss

Let's say you decide you want to buy XYZ Investment Company because you believe it will rise in a nice long uptrend. The stock closed on its last day of trading at $1.00 and you want to purchase the stock when the market opens the next day. Your trading capital is $10,000 and you want to use 20 per cent, or $2,000, to purchase the stock, and set a stop loss of 15 per cent below your buy price. Your stop loss calculation would look like this:

Buy price $1.00 x 15% = $0.15, therefore, your stop loss is your buy price of $1.00 minus $0.15 which equals $0.85.

If the stock closes $0.01 below your stop loss of $0.85 on any day, you would sell the stock to protect capital. Now you need to convert this calculation into actual money, or the trading capital you stand to lose, as you do not want to risk more than 2 per cent of your total capital.

Your calculation would look like this;

- $2,000 x 15% = $300 amount of possible loss

- $300 / $10,000 (total capital) x 100 = 3%.

If you take this trade using a 15 per cent stop loss, you stand to lose 3 per cent of your trading capital. This is above the allowable risk level of no more than 2 per cent of your total capital and is, therefore, unacceptable. Consequently, you need to reduce your stop loss until you reduce your risk level to 2 per cent or below, which, in this example, would equate to a stop loss set at 10 per cent.

The second stop loss you need to work out is the price point where you know with high probability that you are wrong in your analysis. This stop loss is determined using your entry rules. For example, if you bought when a stock crossed above a trend line, you would know your analysis was wrong if the stock traded back down below the lowest low immediately prior to the stock trading above the trend line. This is because a stock in an uptrend continually achieves higher lows or troughs; when it makes a lower low, it suggests that the uptrend is in trouble.

Let's look at an example. In Figure 8.1, opposite, you can see that the lowest low prior to the stock crossing the trend line is $19.61. So if you bought into the stock after it crossed above the downtrend line at $28.70 and then it fell and broke below the low of $19.61, you would stand to lose around 32 per cent, or $633, of your $2,000 trading capital using this stop loss. This is in excess of the 2 per cent allowable risk level, as it equates to over 6 per cent of your total capital of $10,000; therefore, it makes sense to use the percentage stop loss of 10 per cent, as this would enable you to exit the trade with the least amount of loss.

You will notice that the chart opposite is a monthly chart. The stop loss is normally set for price to close below the stop loss before exiting. In most cases, this is the close at the end of the month (on a monthly chart) or the close at the end of the week (if using a weekly chart), although this will depend on the volatility of the stock.

Figure 8.1: Percentage-based stop loss

As you can see in this example, using the 15 per cent stop loss rule allowed the stock to unfold without triggering an exit. While price traded below the stop loss, it did not close below it, which allowed us to remain in the trade and take advantage of the long uptrend.

Once you actually purchase the stock, you need to recalculate the stop loss based on the actual "buy price" you paid to ensure your stop loss is set at the right price point.

Trailing stop loss

Another effective method for preserving your capital is to set a trailing stop loss, which involves raising your stop loss as the price of the stock rises. There are various ways to do this, but probably the best known and one of the easiest methods is to use an uptrend line as your trailing stop loss. As you can see in the chart of Woolworths, Figure 8.2, overleaf, the trend line is following the trend of the stock and providing a trailing stop loss to protect capital. If the stock closed below the trend line, you would sell.

Figure 8.2: Trailing stop loss

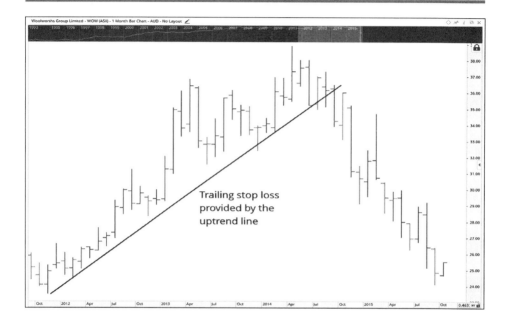

Profit stop loss

It is common practice for people to set profit targets when selling stocks, where the exit is set at a pre-determined level of profit. In my experience, this is done because the individual fears losing the profits they have already made, which stems from the fact:

- They don't have the knowledge to enact a proper plan;

- They don't trust the plan they have; or

- They don't trust themselves to apply the plan properly.

It also explains why people who use this exit strategy generally achieve returns well below their expectations. As the name suggests, a profit stop loss actually stops your profits, which defies the golden rule of letting your profits run. I strongly recommend you do not use this strategy. Always let a stock confirm what it will do before you act, which means to always trade with solid rules that you trust. If you do not trust your rules, then practice until you do.

The market you are trading

Essentially, setting a suitable stop loss really comes down to the volatility of the stock and your investment timeframe. If you are a medium-term investor, your entry and exit strategy would be completed on a weekly chart and you would need to study the stock to determine if it is subject to volatile swings. Nice-trending blue chip stocks are not usually subject to large swings in price over short periods of time when they are at the start of an uptrend, although they do tend to rise for two to four weeks before falling for two to four weeks.

With this in mind, you need to be prepared for the stock to fall for a couple of weeks as it gathers momentum in an uptrend. Setting a stop loss of 10 to 15 per cent for nice-trending blue chip stocks is recommended because anything less than 10 per cent will cause too many false triggers, resulting in losses.

For mid-capped stocks that are subject to larger swings over shorter timeframes, I recommend using a weekly chart to undertake your analysis and setting your stop loss at no more than 10 per cent of your buy price. Falls on mid-cap stocks are usually driven by news; they can fall fairly heavily and very quickly, so you need to preserve your capital. If you are stopped out and the stock starts to rise again, you can always get back in, usually at a lower price.

Probably the easiest thing to remember when setting stop losses is that the quicker the stock moves in price, the more diligent you need to be.

Trading highly leveraged markets such as Forex is, in my opinion, the highest risk trading you can do, contrary to what is portrayed in the marketplace. After nearly two decades of supporting and mentoring traders, it has been my experience that those who attempt to trade these markets, in the illusion that they know how to do so, are those who end up calling out for help, in desperate need of a proper education.

The end result is that they lose most if not all of their capital, which is why stop losses, particularly in these markets, are so important.

To sum up

Remember, preservation of capital is the single most important principle. Placing and enacting stop losses is an area that most people struggle with simply because they associate being stopped out of a trade with being wrong in their analysis; consequently, the guilt of losing money causes them to hold on and ride out a losing stock rather than liquidate and realise a loss.

I cannot stress enough that this is one area in your investment strategy that will either make or break you. Mastering stop losses is one of the most important techniques you can employ to increase your returns. In short, it is about learning how not to lose.

If you find that you are unable to enact your stop losses for whatever reason, I recommend you use a broker who will take a stop loss order for you. It is far better to let someone else handle your trade and preserve your capital if you find you cannot.

Chapter 9

Increasing Your Probability of Success

"The secret to success of every man who has ever been successful...lies in the fact that he formed the habit of doing things that failures don't like to do."

Albert E. N. Gray

No doubt you have been on the kind of road trip where someone inevitably says, "Are we there yet?" If you have never been somewhere before, it is unlikely you will ever get there without a roadmap.

When we don't have a plan, we often live in hope that we won't suffer bad consequences from our actions. This is futile and a complete waste of time. When we know what we are aiming for, we have a much higher chance of success. A plan provides you with the roadmap you need to achieve your financial goals so that you hit the target every time.

In the stock market, your roadmap is your trading plan—a written plan that helps you identify why you are investing and what you want to accomplish. It also provides the basis for your decisions and dictates the actions you need to take when making a profit or loss.

According to the 2014 American Trader Study,[6] 86 per cent of traders agree they are more successful when they stick to their trading plan, and an overwhelming 94 per cent who have a written trading plan agree they are more successful when they stick to it. Given this, would it surprise you to know that only 35 per cent of the survey respondents said they actually have their trading plans written down?

Your roadmap for success

Remember, when we invest, we want to do so with the highest probability of success. With this in mind, and knowing that, as humans, we can become very emotional, we need to develop a set of rules that are measurable, logical and, most importantly, repeatable. I am sorry to say that "gut feel" is not one of those repeatable rules. The rules have to be consistent in their application rather than subjective. The more subjectivity there is, the more our emotions play with our decisions and, consequently, affect the outcome. A well-written trading plan will help overcome this subjectivity and protect your capital.

Trading is about minimising risk, not maximising profit.

Essential elements of a successful trading plan

So, let's consider what you need to include in your trading plan.

- Portfolio type: The portfolio type will determine the appropriate stocks to trade.

  o Remember, in Chapter 3, I provided you with four different types of portfolio based on the level of risk involved. The portfolio you select will also determine the goal of your portfolio, whether it be growth or growth and income.

  o You need to be comfortable with the level of risk you take because one thing is certain: the market will always be there, but you may not if you trade outside your risk tolerance.

- Investment timeframe (term): Your plan must have an appropriate timeframe that suits your lifestyle.

  Do you want to trade over the short, medium, or long term? If you lead a busy lifestyle, I recommend that you select medium to long term as your investment timeframe. A lot of people who lead busy lives attempt to trade short term, however, this is very risky if you do not have the required time to devote to this type of trading.

- Fundamental analysis: You need to document the analysis you undertake that supports your reason to trade. Refer back to Chapter 4 to refresh yourself on how to select stocks using this technique.

- Trading rules: You need to clearly document your buy and sell rules in your trading plan. We discuss this in more detail shortly.

- Money management: This area of your trading plan is one of the most important aspects to consider when trading.

  o You must know how much you intend to invest in any one trade. Remember, Golden Rule #3 states that you should never invest more than 20 per cent of your total capital in any one stock, therefore, the amount you invest is relative to the number of stocks you hold. For example, if you decide to hold between 8 and 12 stocks, you would invest between 12 and 8 per cent (respectively) of your total capital in any one stock.

  o How much are you willing to risk on each trade? You must set a stop loss or an exit price in case price falls after you enter the trade. Remember, for stocks, this is usually 10 to 15 per cent below your purchase price depending on the volatility of the stock.

     You should also look at the actual dollar amount you are investing and ask yourself, honestly, "Am I comfortable risking that much?"

- Risk level: What is your risk tolerance?

There is an undeniable link between risk and knowledge. The more risk you take, the higher the level of knowledge required to manage the risk.

Risk tolerance is the degree of risk you are willing to take with your investments. Usually, the higher the risk, the higher the expected return. In some cases, the risk is almost zero and, in other cases, the risk is very high. For example, investing in a term deposit is virtually risk free and requires almost no knowledge. Investing in the stock market, however, involves a higher degree of risk, which, therefore, requires a much higher level of knowledge and skill.

Understanding your tolerance to risk will help maximise your wealth creation potential. I always recommend that an individual's comfort level regarding risk should be determined by what I like to call the "sleep factor". In other words, you should only ever consider investing in assets that allow you to sleep at night. Believe me—it is far better to sleep than worry about how your investments are performing.

You need to consider whether your tolerance to risk is low, medium or high. Asking this question will help to determine the risk you are willing to take and how much money you will invest. When answering this question, you need to consider your current level of knowledge and experience in the market, so that you do not take on too much risk.

You need to use a trading plan every time you intend to buy a stock, as it will assist you to formalise your thoughts while you analyse whether the stock fits with the overall goal of your portfolio. The plan also helps manage your risk, as you are aware how much money you are willing to lose if the stock falls in value. You may even discover once you complete your analysis that the stock is not worth owning, which you may not have known had you not undertaken the analysis and documented your intentions.

So, let's look at how you might apply this trading plan to your investment strategy.

Your share trading plan

Let's say you decide you want to invest in a growth portfolio and your preference is to trade over the medium to long term in stocks that produce both capital growth and income, although, because you are operating a growth portfolio, your preference is for growth stocks.

You notice that BHP would be a good stock to add to your portfolio because it has achieved record growth in recent times. Fundamentally, the stock has been undervalued, as the price earnings ratio is fourteen while the market average is twenty. In addition, the earnings per share has grown from the previous year and it is expected that this will continue. You know this means that the share price should rise over the medium term, if not longer. To confirm your choice, you review the stock chart to determine whether it is trending up to maximise your chances of success.

Confirming the trend

Remember, the first step in your analysis is to determine where the stock is and where it has been in order to determine where it will go. When trading over the longer term, you are looking for the short and medium-term direction to be up and the longer-term direction to be down, as we want to enter the stock near the start of a longer-term uptrend. Obviously, if we waited for the long-term uptrend to be confirmed, we could end up entering mid-way through or at the end of an uptrend, which would limit our profit potential. Because the long-term direction is the most important factor with this type of trade, you need to use a monthly chart to analyse the stock and the trend.

When trading over the medium term, we are looking for confirmation that the short and medium-term trend are up, with the longer-term trend being of no real significance because we are trading a trend of lesser degree within the longer-term trend. Indeed, you will often find that you can trade two or three medium-term trends within a longer-term trend. Because the medium-term direction is the most important, we must use a weekly and monthly chart to analyse the stock and the trend.

I have developed a trading plan, Figure 9.1, overleaf, which encompasses each of the elements you need to consider when buying and selling stocks.

Figure 9.1: Share trading plan

Portfolio Type:	*Growth*	Date of trade:	*1/02/20XX*
Goal:	*Growth and income*	Buy price:	*$31.35*
Term:	*Medium to long term*	Trade number:	*02/20XX*
Stock name:	*BHP Billiton*	Code:	*BHP*

Fundamental Analysis

	Stock	Market average	Additional notes
PE ratio:	*14*	*20*	*BHP achieved*
Dividend yield:	*3%*	*3%*	*record growth last*
% Franked:	*100%*		*quarter and this*
			looks set to continue

EPS: *Last year: 25   Current: 34   Expected: 54*

Trading Rules

Entry rules

Exit rules

Trend lines	Yes No	**Trend lines**	Yes No
Has the stock formed two consecutive closes above a downtrend line?	☐ ☐	Has the stock formed two consecutive closes below an uptrend line?	☐ ☐
		Stop loss	Yes No
		Has the stock traded through the 15% stop loss?	☐ ☐

Money Management

Total capital:	*$100,000*
% of capital for purchase:	*12%*
Position size:	*$12,000*
No. of shares:	*382*
Brokerage costs:	*$20*
Total cost of trade:	*$11,995.70*

Risk Calculation:

Stop loss		Calculation
15% of buy price:	*$4.70*	*$12,000 x 15% = $1,800*
Stop loss:	*$26.65*	*$1,800/$100,000 = 1.8%*
Exit price:	*$26.64*	**This should not exceed 2%**

Figure 9.1: Share trading plan (cont'd)

Notes:

_____

_____

_____

_____

_____

Psychology rules:

_____

_____

_____

_____

Attach a chart of your analysis to this trading plan

So, let's discuss each of the elements in more detail.

Entry and exit signals

When trading over the longer term, your actual entry and exit points, while important, are not critical to your analysis, as we are expecting the trade to last around two to three years. This also applies when trading over the medium term, as we are expecting the trade to last from around three to eighteen months. This means entering or exiting a trade a few days or even weeks late will generally make very little difference to your overall profitability.

When determining your trading rules, you need to phrase each one so as to elicit a yes/no answer. As you are buying a stock that is trending up, your entry signal would read like this:

Buy: Has the stock formed two consecutive closes above a downtrend line (if trading on a weekly chart, for example)?

When setting your exit rules, remember you need to set an initial stop loss in the event the trade turns sour after you enter, as well as an exit rule for when the stock is in profit. Taking this into account, your exit signals would be as follows:

Sell: Has the stock traded 15 per cent below my buy price or has the stock formed two consecutive closes below an uptrend line (if trading on a weekly chart, for example)?

Money management

Once your entry rules are triggered, you need to work out your money management rules before placing a trade to ensure you do not take on too much risk. When calculating a stop loss, you need to use the most recent price available to determine your "buy price", which will be the closing price for the previous day or week.

Let's say your total capital is $100,000 and you decide you would prefer to hold eight stocks in your portfolio. The maximum you can invest in any one stock is, therefore, 12 per cent, or $12,000, of your total capital.

Managing the risk

You now need to calculate the amount you are willing to lose or how far you will allow the stock to fall before you exit. To do this, you take the buy price and multiply it by the percentage stop loss. You then take the stop loss amount and subtract it from the buy price to arrive at your stop loss target.

Given that, in this example, we are using a 15 per cent stop loss, you need to multiply the buy price of $31.35 by 15 per cent ($31.35 x 15% = $4.70) and then subtract this from the buy price to arrive at your stop loss target ($31.35 – $4.70 = $26.65). Hence, if the stock trades $0.01 below $26.65 on any day, you will exit the trade to protect capital. Remember, once you actually purchase the stock, you need to recalculate your stop loss based on the actual buy price you pay to ensure your stop loss is set at the right price point.

You also need to calculate the level of risk you are willing to take before you enter a trade. Using a position size of $12,000, this represents 1.80 per cent of your total capital of $100,000 ($12,000 x 15% / $100,000 x 100 = 1.80%), which is within the allowable risk level of no more than two per cent.

It is also important, when considering money management, that you do not expose yourself to much risk. Therefore, once you hold between 5 and 12 stocks, you should consider increasing the size of each position you hold rather than increasing the number of stocks you hold. For example, if your portfolio has increased to $120,000, you could invest up to $14,400, or 12 per cent, of your total portfolio in the next stock you buy, if it is your intention to continue holding eight stocks.

Another method you can use that will compound your returns is to invest the same percentage of your portfolio each time you purchase a stock. However, once again, you would never invest more than 20 per cent of your total portfolio in any one stock. For example, let's assume you now have $120,000 in your portfolio; you want to invest 15 per cent in a stock and so buy shares worth $18,000. If you make 30 per cent in profit on the stock, your total portfolio would be $123,400 (excluding costs). Therefore, the next time you buy shares, you would still invest 15 per cent of your total portfolio, but this time it would mean an investment of $18,510. Can you see how this method compounds your returns?

Notes and psychology

In this area of your trading plan, you would make notes about why you are taking the trade. It is a good idea to get into the habit of documenting this information, as it can act as a valuable learning tool when a trade turns bad. You may also want to document why you have sold the stock when the time arises.

You also need to document your psychology rules, as well as your frame of mind, at the time of the trade. For example, you may state in your trading plan that you never make decisions while the market is open or that you will never trade if you feel anxious or under stress. You can write whatever rules are most applicable to you; everyone is different.

The information you provide in your trading plan will assist you with the paperwork you need to maintain for taxation purposes when buying and selling stocks, which we cover in more detail later in this chapter. For now, let's look at how you would manage your trade.

Managing your trade

Your exposure to risk in the stock market is greatest when you first purchase a stock simply because you pay brokerage, which means you are at a loss the moment you buy. While your trading plan may indicate there is a high probability you will succeed, there is no certainty you will make a profit. It is only when the stock begins to rise in price that these risks diminish. Therefore, once you enter the stock market, you need to manage these risks.

Now that you have implemented safe money management practices and set your stop loss to minimise any risk, what else can you do? As you are trading over the medium to long term, I recommend you look at the price of the stock at the end of the week to see if it has traded below your stop loss. I generally find the best time to look at stocks is on the weekend when the market has closed, as you are in a more relaxed state and able to make unemotional decisions. This will also eliminate any reactive emotions you may expose yourself to when viewing the stock during the week when the market is open. Once the stock is in profit, you only need to look at it at the end of each week to determine if it has fulfilled your sell rules.

I can hear some of you saying, "But what happens if the stock falls during the week?" If I had a dollar for every time I stopped someone reacting to the market during the week, I would have a very healthy piggy bank. Short-term fluctuations in the price of a stock are normal, which is why I recommend you wait to view the closing price at the end of the week; this way, you will have a much better perspective on how the stock is performing. Remember, once the stock is in profit, your risk is minimised.

When using trend lines to exit a stock, you may not be able to draw a valid uptrend line for quite some time after entering. To protect capital in the event that the stock turns and falls, you could draw a two-point trend line when the opportunity arises, although, you need to remember this is not a valid trend line; rather, it is an indication that you may need to exit in the absence of any valid trend line. If the stock continued to trade down after three consecutive months (on a monthly chart) or twelve consecutive weeks (on a weekly chart), I would sell because this would indicate that a medium to long-term downtrend is in place and further falls are likely.

The trick to medium and long-term trading is to have patience and confidence in your trading plan. In my experience, most mistakes in trading relate to how you manage your trades or what you do after you enter. Individuals unsure where to exit tend to exit too early because they want to protect profits, only to find that the stock continues to rise. Or they exit too late because they believe they were right in their analysis and won't admit they made a mistake or that the trade has simply gone against them. The catchcry is always, "I will lose too much if I exit now!" Hmm…which loss would you rather? Ten per cent, 20 per cent, 50 per cent or more?

Remember—if you stick to your trading plan, you will have a greater chance of making rational decisions rather than reactive decisions. Unless a stock tells you to sell by triggering one of your exit signals, do not sell. I promise you, if you follow your plan, you won't fall into the trap of becoming an average investor, which means you will be far more profitable and successful in the long run.

Paperwork

This is the final piece in your plan and should be completed after you purchase the stock. Unfortunately, many people run into difficulties when it comes to completing their paperwork, usually because they don't have an effective system in place. I suggest, if you are not good at handling your paperwork, that you give it to someone who is. My wife is very good at keeping track of things and being organised, so having her do my paperwork not only keeps things in perfect order, it minimises the chance of mistakes being compounded.

For example, a good friend of mine ended up buying more stock when her intention was to sell. Luckily, her partner checked the contract notes later that day and realised that not only had she not sold the stock, but that she now owned twice as much—and as the stock was falling in price, she was losing twice as much. This sort of thing can and does happen, therefore, you need to be diligent in order to minimise these types of mistakes.

I have created a simple spreadsheet in Excel to provide you with an example of how you can maintain your paperwork. This sheet is called a trading log and needs to be completed each time you place your money in the stock market. Your trading log should list all transactions that take place during the period you hold a stock, which includes all dividend payments. The document should be stored with your contract notes and trading plan in a folder so you can refer to them whenever you need to. Always make sure you check your contract notes as you receive them to confirm you have bought and sold what you intended.

As shown in Figure 9.2, overleaf, each transaction is placed on a separate line. The first line refers to the information in your trading plan. For example, you enter the details in the first line after purchasing shares in BHP. When you receive a dividend, you make another entry in your trading log, and so on, until you finally sell the stock.

Figure 9.2: Trading log

Code	Buy/Sell	Trade No.	Date of Transaction	No. of Shares	Price	Brokerage	Total Amount	Dividend	Profit/Loss	Total
BHP	Buy	Feb-XX	01/02/20XX	382	$31.35	$20.00	$11,995.70			
BHP	Dividend		27/09/20XX					$880.00		
BHP	Sell		14/06/20XX	382	$39.80	$20.00	$15,203.60		$3,207.90	$4,087.90

Determining your profitability

If you were dropped into the middle of the desert and had to find your way out, what would be the first thing you needed to know? Obviously, where you are! If you don't know where you are, it doesn't matter what the destination is because you won't be able to plan your journey. Learning to trade is a journey and it is important as you travel along this path that you know you are heading towards your destination—in the stock market, this destination is your overall profitability.

Given this, those who are successful know two important figures: the first is their win/loss ratio and the second is their profit/loss ratio. These important figures are derived from the statistics you keep each time you trade. Once you know these figures, you know exactly where you are in your trading journey, and you can work out whether you need to adjust anything to ensure you arrive at your destination.

Win/loss ratio

You derive the win/loss ratio from the records you keep of your trades, which is why it is important to keep your paperwork up to date. To calculate your win/loss ratio, you simply add up all winning trades and all losing trades and then compare them.

For example, if for every five trades, you win three and lose two, your win/loss ratio would be 3:2. You may find you have a ratio of 2:3 or 4:1. Whatever the figure, when you combine this with your profit/loss ratio, it will tell you whether you are profitable.

When expressing the win/loss ratio as a percentage, you calculate the number of winning trades, divide it by the total number of trades and multiply by 100. For example, if your win/loss ratio is 3:2, this represents five trades in total, with three being winning trades. Therefore, you would divide three by five and multiply it by 100 to arrive at 60 per cent.

Profit/loss ratio

The profit/loss ratio is also derived from the paperwork you keep and is determined by the profit and/or loss you make on each trade. You need to turn the profit or loss you make on each trade into a percentage. To do this, you simply divide the amount you invested by the profit or loss you made and then multiply it by 100.

For example, if you invested $15,000 and sold a month later, taking $17,000 out of the market, you generated a profit of $2,000. You would divide the profit of $2,000 by the initial investment of $15,000 multiplied by 100 to arrive at 13.33 per cent. You need to do this each time you trade.

You then add up all of the percentage profits and divide by the number of trades to arrive at your average profit figure. You then repeat this process for your losses until you arrive at an average loss figure. These figures will tell you how much profit, on average, you make on a winning trade and the average loss you make on a losing trade.

For example, in Table 9.1, below, we have shown the results of ten trades, seven of which are profitable and three of which resulted in losses. The total percentage of the winning trades is 111 per cent. If we divide this figure by seven (the number of profitable trades), we arrive at an average profit of 15.86 per cent. The three losing trades total 28 per cent. If we divide this figure by three, we arrive at an average loss of 9 per cent. Using these figures, we now have a more realistic view of how profitable we really are.

Table 9.1: Average profit versus average loss

Trades	1	2	3	4	5	6	7	8	9	10	Total	Average
Profitable Trades	3		9	18	13			35	6	27	111%	15.86%
Losing Trades		-9				-13	-6				-28%	-9%

Determining your overall profitability

Now you need to combine your win/loss ratio and profit/loss ratio to determine whether you are profitable. An individual with a win/loss ratio of 4:1 sounds impressive and, on the surface, you would think they are profitable. But let's look at an example.

If your win loss ratio is 4:1 and your profit/loss ratio is 10 per cent profit and 50 per cent loss, this indicates you win four times out of five with a profit of 10 per cent and you lose one time out of five with a loss of 50 per cent. Therefore, you gained 40 per cent and lost 50 per cent over five trades, which is an unprofitable trading system because your net result is minus 2 per cent (as demonstrated below).

While we touched on this in a previous chapter, it is important to reiterate the point. Let's assume you have total capital of $50,000 and your position size for each trade is $10,000.

- 4 winning trades x $10,000 = $40,000

- $40,000 x 10% profit = $4,000

- 1 losing trade x $10,000 = $10,000

- $10,000 x 50% loss = $5,000

- Total: $4,000 profit – $5,000 loss = ($1,000)

- Percentage loss calculation = ($1,000)/$50,000 x 100 = –2%

Don't fall into the trap of believing you can never go broke taking a profit! As the above example proves, this is simply not true. If you trade with profit targets in mind (which I strongly discourage) and you have a profit target of 15 per cent, meaning you exit the trade or take profits at 15 per cent, then even with an excellent win/loss ratio of 4:1, you will still lose if you have a 65 per cent loss. If, on the other hand, you allowed your profits to run, you could average a higher return, resulting in a profitable trading plan.

So, let's consider the overall profitability of the portfolio we traded in Chapter 6. In total, we placed 61 trades over the ten-year period. At the end of 2016, we were still holding eight trades, all of which were in profit (refer back to page 114). So, we completed fifty-three trades, of which thirty-six were winning trades, resulting in an average profit of 33.24 per cent, with the largest gain achieved on Macquarie with a profit of 139.78 per cent in 2014. The remaining seventeen trades were losing trades, resulting in an average loss of 8.15 per cent, with the largest loss on a trade 15.28 per cent. The completed trades are detailed in Table 9.2, opposite.

Table 9.2: Overall profitability of the portfolio traded in Chapter 6

Total Trades	Winning Trades	Losing Trades	Open Trades	Win/Loss Ratio	Average Profit on Winning Trades	Average Loss on Losing Trades
61	36	17	8	67.92%	33.24%	8.15%

As you can see, the win/loss ratio on all closed trades is 67.92 per cent, which is quite impressive given that many people struggle to achieve greater than 50 per cent profitable trades. If we included the remaining eight trades, our win/loss ratio would increase to well over 70 per cent. Remember, this outcome was achieved using very simple rules for buying and selling over the long term, which verifies a number of important lessons that I have shared with you throughout this book:

- Many people believe they need to trade more frequently and over shorter timeframes to make good money; this example demonstrates that this is simply not true.

- Many people also believe they need to use complex rules or computer-generated algorithms to achieve solid profits, which I have also demonstrated is not the case.

- Many traders hold the mistaken belief that they need to set very tight stop losses. This is also untrue, as highlighted by the win/loss ratio we achieved. In short, by setting a 15 per cent stop loss, we were able to trade less and make more money.

To sum up

As I have said multiple times throughout this book, one of the golden rules of trading is to let your profits run and cut your losses short. So, when you decide to take profits, be careful not to cut your profits short; this could dramatically affect the overall results of your trading success.

People will happily tell you their win/loss ratio having never bothered to calculate their profit or loss; they are fooling not only themselves but also those they share this information with. In fact, if they calculated these figures, most would be shocked to find out how much they are actually losing from trading. Do not fall into this trap. It is imperative that you regularly calculate these figures, so that you can manage yourself and your trading.

Now that you understand how to implement your roadmap to success in the stock market, let's consider how trading the stock market can create you a lifestyle, rather than becoming your lifestyle.

Chapter 10

Trading for a Lifestyle

"Life isn't about finding yourself. Life is about creating yourself!"

George Bernard Shaw

"We learn from our mistakes," so the saying goes, but if that is true, why do people continually make the same mistakes believing things will turn out differently?

Some time ago, I received an all too familiar phone call. It was a gentleman who had been investing in the stock market. Having made some money, he told me he was going to take six months' long service leave and trade options in an effort to become a full-time trader, so he would not have to go back to work.

Other than having read a couple of books, he had no education in the stock market and had simply made money in a very bullish market. This is a common theme among traders who believe they are invincible after taking profits from the stock market over a short period of time, particularly when the market is bullish. So, what do you think his chances were of becoming a successful trader if he took his long service leave and did nothing more to educate himself?

Statistically, anyone trading options has less than a 5 per cent chance of being successful in the long term, but that aside, even if he were to trade stocks, what do you think his chances would have been? At best guess, I would have said less than 50 per cent, although, if I am to be truly honest, I believe it would be less than 30 per cent.

If it is your intention to create a lifestyle from trading, you need to follow the "Be, Do, Have" principle. You need to BE a full-time trader, DO what a full-time trader does and then you will HAVE what a full-time trader has.

How to trade for a lifestyle

It can take up to two years for anyone to become a full-time trader, if not longer. Knowledge is everything in the context of trading. Remember, the streets are littered with wannabe traders and, in a bull market, many are profitable through sheer luck rather than sound knowledge.

To be a full-time trader, you need to combine a high level of knowledge and skill with experience; without this, your probability of success over the long term is very low. When you leave work to trade full time, you no longer have the security of a regular income; this means your attention is often focused on making profits from every trade to pay the bills.

This need for survival often results in the trader trying to trade more to make up for any trading losses. A spiral of increased pressure begins, resulting in the trader taking higher risks to get back on top. Unfortunately, because of their lack of knowledge and experience, many end up back at work.

Being a full-time trader does not mean you replace one job with another and work every day. It simply means that your trading is paying for your lifestyle. This is a very important distinction and one I suggest you ponder if your goal is to trade full time. Trading is about creating a lifestyle, not making it your lifestyle.

Hence, if your goal is to replace your income of $100,000 a year, it does not mean you have to make around $2,000 a week from trading. It just means your total trading profits over one year need to equate to $100,000. Looking at it like that, rather than adopting the micro-view of needing to generate $2,000 a week, will make a dramatic difference to your psychology and how you trade the market.

Trading is about creating a lifestyle, not making it your lifestyle.

Capital and percentage return

Another very important point is that you should only subject yourself to the amount of risk you need to achieve your goal(s). For example, if you have $500,000 to invest and you need an income of $50,000 a year, you only need a return of 10 per cent. Just buying the top blue chip stocks for the medium to longer term should deliver this income in a reasonable market.

If you only have $100,000 to invest and you still require $50,000 in income a year, you will need to generate a 50 per cent return on your capital. Therefore, you will need to trade stocks that assist you in producing this return or use leveraging in your trading plan.

If your goal is to trade full time, I highly recommend you prove to yourself that you can not only trade but also make the sort of income you want from trading while still working. And you should do this for an absolute minimum of six months although, twelve months is preferable. Now, I can hear some of you saying, "But if I give up work I will have more time to trade and, therefore, I will naturally get better returns." My response to this is: prove it. It simply does not work that way.

If you can replace your income by trading while still in a full-time job, not only will your confidence increase but you will also have built up a sum of money to draw upon when you do finally go full time. Having this "safety" margin is one of the smartest plans you can have, and it is one of the main strategies for building wealth.

Fail safe

What exactly is a "safety margin"? It is simply a fail safe—in case things go wrong. For example, if you use leveraging to invest, you could avoid using all of the available funds that the lender provides. If you want to trade for a lifestyle, then having a safety margin means having enough cash in the bank to sustain your lifestyle for at least six to twelve months. This will give you more options when something does go wrong.

All too often, I see traders attempting to trade full time without enough cash to support themselves end up trading short term and taking higher risks. This only results in making trading decisions based on the need to derive an income rather than on good trading techniques. Consequently, they end up exiting trades when they should hold or entering trades in the hope of a quick profit. You should never place yourself in the position of relying on emotional decisions; this is a trader's greatest downfall.

One of the biggest misconceptions about trading for a lifestyle is that you need to trade short term. If your capital limits you to trading this timeframe, I suggest you revert to my original proposed strategy of trading while working full time. Failure to do so will place you at high risk of losing your capital and ending up back at work regardless.

In the lead up to the GFC, I remember receiving a phone call from an individual asking for help. He had given up work to trade full time after a few wins in a bull market, but he now found he was not doing very well. After I asked some questions, it became obvious that he was not following his trading rules but, rather, making emotional decisions in order to extract some cash flow from his trades on a weekly basis. The best advice I could give him was to go back to work to earn money, while at the same time prove to himself he could be consistently profitable before contemplating this lifestyle.

Portfolio set up

The best way to set yourself up if you want to trade full time is to follow Golden Rule #4, as outlined in Chapter 3: allocate 90 per cent of your capital to a medium to long-term portfolio that will perform year in, year out, and allocate the remaining 10 per cent to short-term trading to generate cash flow. This rule ensures you are protecting your capital by not subjecting the majority of it to high-risk trades. Remember, the amount you allocate to short-term trading does not have to replace your income; it only has to supplement your total portfolio.

For example, if you have $200,000 in capital and you need to make $50,000 in income, your asset allocation would be $180,000 in a safe, medium-term portfolio, with the average trade length between seven and eighteen months. If you averaged a 12 per cent return on this portfolio each year including dividends, you would receive $21,600, which means you only need to make $28,400 from your short-term trading account. Therefore, the $20,000 in capital allocated to your short-term trading needs to generate, on average, just over $2,366 per month. Let me explain.

Now let's assume you decide to use leveraging to trade short term, which, in some markets, allows you to leverage ten times your capital. This means you would have $200,000 to invest in your short term trading account. Therefore, if you trade a stock using leverage, it only has to rise around 1.50 per cent in a month for you to make around $2,366 per month, assuming you only invest 80 per cent of your available capital ($160,000) for short-term trading in four leveraged positions. This is very achievable and, more importantly, very repeatable for someone who has acquired the knowledge and skill and has the experience.

Some instruments, such as Forex, allow you to trade on a margin of 1 or 2 per cent, although this is not recommended unless you are extremely proficient as a trader and have the time and knowledge to manage this risk. That said, if you allocated $20,000 to trade on a margin of 1 percent, you would have $2 million in your short-term trading account. To achieve the same return trading on a margin of 10:1, all you need to do is move the decimal point by one place, which means the trade only needs to rise around 0.15 per cent in a month for you to make around $2,366 per month. Again, this assumes you have only invested 80 per cent of your available capital for short-term trading in four leveraged positions.

Consider going part time

People often want to trade the stock market because they are sick of working full time and desire a change in their lifestyle. Getting up at 6.00am is not exactly exciting, especially when working for a company that does not pay well or appreciate your efforts. If it is your desire to have the profits from your trading pay for your lifestyle, I recommend you transition to trading full time by working part time, rather than giving up work entirely. This has huge benefits, as your psychology will slowly adjust to being less dependent on a steady income stream.

Working part time will also allow you to transition to a life of deriving your income from trading. Funnily enough, people find they actually crave work again after they leave.

At my recent Art of Trading workshop, a client shared how he was in the process of decluttering his life, while transitioning to trading for a lifestyle. He had reduced his hours at work and, on his days off, he was honing his trading skills to enable him to replace his income in its entirety. He also shared that, in the process, he was selling things he did not need and downsizing his living arrangements so he could travel and enjoy the benefits of his new lifestyle.

It's worth mentioning, however, that trading for a lifestyle is not for everyone; it can be lonely—you are home alone while your friends are at work and this can lead to boredom. Some people I know have taken up hobbies or charity work to keep themselves occupied, while others have gone back to work, even though they were successful in generating sufficient income from their trading to maintain their lifestyle. Before you leap, it is important to consider the changes that will occur to your lifestyle.

The transition to trading for a lifestyle is a journey; it is not something that happens overnight. Some people find when they get there that it is the best thing that they have ever done, but others find it is not for them. Whether you ultimately decide to trade for a lifestyle or not, the most important point is that you enjoy and profit from the journey.

The emotions of trading and how to manage them with a mechanical trading system

You have heard me say throughout this book that you should trade the markets objectively, unemotionally and with the discipline to consistently apply your trading strategy. This may be relatively easy to do when analysing the markets outside of trading hours. But how do you stay calm, focused, objective and unemotional while under pressure, in a real-time trading environment?

Irrespective of your chosen timeframe when trading, it is common for traders, especially those new to trading, to watch the market on a daily basis. I strongly discourage this, as it subjects the trader to the emotions of the market and the possibility of being influenced by the current day's activity when making decisions. But how do you minimise the downside of this practice?

What follows is the true story of a full-time trader who traded (note the past tense) short term, overnight on international markets. While this may not be your style, the methodology presented and the lessons learnt are transferrable to any market over any timeframe.

The trader's methodology

Remember, to be able to maintain a disciplined and consistent approach to your trading psychology, it is important to develop a sound set of written trading rules using a mechanical trading system. This will assist you to keep human emotions out of your trading decisions. As we have discussed throughout this book, it is important to do the following:

- Develop a written trading plan that is compatible with your own psychological make-up and includes your psychology rules.

- Develop the confidence in yourself to be able to consistently apply your trading strategy calmly and without fear or hesitation.

- Before you enter a trade, determine whether it meets your trading rules. Calculate your risk/reward ratio. Calculate the maximum risk exposure of your trading capital according to stringent money management rules and write down your stop loss exit point for the trade.

- Gain an understanding for how the stock responds to any news or announcements. Understand the volatility of the markets that you are trading. Adjust your position size so that stops are placed outside of the daily noise of the markets.

- Once you enter the trade, evaluate the "what if" scenarios that could come out of leftfield and have a strategy that allows you to act immediately, without reservation or hesitation.

A case study

Despite a consistent and sound trading methodology, reality can sometimes bite the best of us. What follows is a real-life situation that a trader shared with me; it contains some pertinent trading messages that we can all learn from. (Any underlining in the case study is that of the trader.)

At the start of the new financial year, I decided to try a new trading strategy. I only traded on a $50K account (1 per cent margin = $5M positions can be opened on the Contracts for Difference (CFD) indices I trade), and every time the account reached $55K, I removed $5K and transferred it into a non-trading account. My other new rule was that I stopped trading for the remainder of the week once my profit objective had been reached (or, as a bonus, I would only then trade small positions with very tight stops and carry the remaining profits into the next week).

I had successfully employed this strategy every week for two months by not using any more than about $10,000 of my available funds—averaging about 35 to 40 per cent profit per trade. I had employed strict and unwavering discipline, sound money management principles and kept a level, rational head. I only made "businessman decisions" and only took "businessman risks". Every day, I continually repeated my mantra: "I am so happy and grateful now that I am a successful, profitable and disciplined trader, consistently taking profits every week, etc."

But then Friday night came along...and I threw all rationale out the window. I had already surpassed my profit objective for the week (and, hence, had no reason to even trade again that week) and had transferred profits out of the trading account the day before. Maybe there was a full moon or something, maybe it was impatience *as I wanted to double my trading profits (sick of trying to be a tortoise when I really wanted to be the fast and furious hare), but I decided to trade on Friday night "just for the hell of it" and ignored my own adage: "Remember to trade WELL—NOT often."*

I shorted the DAX on the first half hour's low on Friday night (impatient = should have waited for first hour to get confirmation of the direction of the market)...but the market decided to go up instead. I didn't exit as I believed the DAX would come off...so I "averaged down my loss" by shorting another 100 contracts (= naughty, naughty)...and, of course, the markets kept rising and rising (obviously trying to tell me something—but I chose not to listen to what the market was *trying to tell me). In immense pain (stress and anxiety), I halved my position before the US opened in case the US rallied too much—dragging the DAX with it. It was a volatile morning session on US open (as usual) so I closed out the DAX position on any pull backs = ($11,000) loss.*

So what next? Call it a night and go away and lick my wounds over the weekend and reassess where I went wrong? Of course not (that would be tooooooooo sensible)—what does any "brain-dead" trader do when they take a big hit? <u>Try to win it back, of course</u>! So I went long on the SPX500 (as I now believed I got the markets wrong = <u>lack of faith in my own analysis</u>). Naturally, the US markets decided to range all night—whip-sawing me in and out of long and short positions (and increasing my losses, pain and frustration).

I could have taken small profits along the way on the SPX500 (which I would have done happily if I wasn't carrying a big loss)—but no—I wanted my "blood money" back and was hanging out for that elusive "<u>big hit</u>" that would win me back all of my lost money (plus more) = commonly referred to as "<u>taking revenge on the markets</u>" (another brain-dead strategy). I then took a huge short position on SPX500 (<u>ignoring sound, unemotional and rational money management practices</u>) in the US afternoon session, "<u>hoping</u>" for the US markets to tank like the DAX eventually did (yes—the DAX closed heavily south and would have put me in a $10,000 profit <u>if I had stuck with my convictions</u> = such is life = get over it and move on, the past is the past, etc. etc.)

And the US finally finished on its high for the day (surprise, surprise), leaving me with no option but to close out half of my short position in the last five minutes of trade—and now holding 1,000 SPX500 short contracts for Monday, "<u>hoping and praying</u>" that the markets come off (if not—I'll take my hit and close out ASAP when markets reopen on Monday). I eventually went to bed at 7:00am Saturday morning, a rather shattered and distraught little puppy dog!

So the net loss from my irrational/emotional and misguided (read: brain-dead) one night's trading frenzy effectively wiped out <u>ALL</u> of the financial year's profits!

Do you people out there hear my message loud and clear? Does this sound all tooooooooo familiar? I have personally repeated the above nightmare numerous times over the past couple of years, costing me somewhere between $500K-$1M. And I am still waiting for the time that I learn from my mistakes—once and for all! It is definitely <u>not</u> good enough to be 90 per cent disciplined in this game (especially when using high leverage in volatile markets)—you have to be 110 per cent disciplined or stay out of the game! It may only take a moment's distraction to undo all of the good work you have so diligently been doing!

I'm the one who usually preaches to others about applying sound money management, stopping losses quickly, taking profits whenever the markets present them, sound trading psychology, consistency and discipline, blah, blah, blah. And, yes, I've read and re-read all of the rules too! But I will be revisiting the rules again—and doing a lot more soul searching.

Sorry, but I am only human. I may be the "90 per cent man"—but in this game you need to be 110 per cent plus, all of the time, to produce <u>consistent results</u>.

I will regroup and regain my composure for Monday's trading session and will then calmly, unemotionally and rationally make a businessman's decision, depending on what the markets tell me.

Trust you can all gain some wisdom from my pain and suffering.

Trade safely!

This situation is not uncommon. I have met many traders who have lost $500,000 to $1 million in much the same fashion, and dozens more who have lost $50,000 to $100,000 plus. Some of these traders were excellent technicians of their craft, while others were simply a car crash waiting to happen. We have all been affected, to some degree, by the same emotions that this trader experienced. So what are the lessons we can learn from this?

Lessons we can learn

There are a number of important points that can be taken from the above case study:

- Even an experienced and (usually) disciplined trader using a proven trading system can still get caught up with the emotions of trading (especially trading volatile markets), and the best of intentions can go horribly wrong. It is important that you always endeavour to keep your psychology in check and not get caught up in the emotional roller coaster ride of the market's highs and lows. You must continually strive to trade from a balanced, unbiased, objective and detached perspective.

- It is imperative to use and stick to a sound, written trading plan using a mechanical trading system that helps eliminate your emotions from the trading decision process. The greatest obstacle to confidently and consistently implementing a trading strategy is the individual themselves.

- You need to develop the patience to employ your written trading plan. Don't jump the gun or second guess the market's direction before your trading plan has given you a clear signal to enter (or exit) a trade.

- Before entering a trade, you must know your entry and exit strategy and have thought about a contingency plan in case the markets don't respond the way you anticipate. You do not want to be caught off guard and have to make trading decisions in the heat of the moment. Plan the trade—and then trade the plan!

- Never over-trade. You are in the business of trading the stock market to make a profit—not for the excitement of the game. You shouldn't trade just for the sake of trading—because you are bored, you think that the market owes you something or you think you have to. If your trading plan does not present a signal to enter a trade, stand aside and patiently wait for a signal to be generated. Don't go looking for trades that may not be there. You should never exit a position just because you have lost patience or open a position just because you have become anxious from waiting. Remember to trade well—not often!

- Always use sound money management principles and never place too much money in any one position, no matter how sure you are of the trade. The number one priority in trading is to protect your capital at all costs so that you live to fight another day.

- Never average down a loss or try to win back a losing trade. It is always better to accept a loss, calmly close out of that position, then patiently sit back and watch the markets for another possible entry, in a rational and emotionally detached frame of mind. In the above case study, the individual should have determined his stop loss exit point before he entered the trade and accepted that if that stop was triggered, the timing or analysis for that trade was incorrect. The worst mistake you can make is to add to a losing trade, hoping that the market will turn around and go in your favour (it rarely does). The more you add to a losing position, the more you become emotionally attached to the outcome, which produces unnecessary stress and anxiety. Eventually, your psychology is thrown way out of balance and it becomes more difficult to act rationally and make business-like decisions.

- Accept that losses are an integral part of trading. If your trading plan indicates that, over a period of time, it will achieve a 75 per cent win/loss ratio—then accept the fact that, on average, every fourth trade will not be profitable. Have faith in your trading system and act on the buy and sell signals that are generated. The objective is to incur only small losses, by cutting your losses quickly, and let your profits run, by staying in winning trades for as long as your trading strategy permits. Put any loss behind you, move on and get over it. Period! Focus on the present moment (not the past) and then concentrate on looking for the next potentially profitable trade that your trading plan generates.

To sum up

The key to consistent, profitable and successful trading is to develop a proven mechanical trading system that minimises human input and eliminates emotions from the trading decision process. You must learn to keep your psychology in check so that you don't get caught up in emotionally driven decisions. You must develop strict discipline, sound money management principles and self-confidence in your trading abilities.

Before you place a trade, it is prudent to think through the whole trading process. Write down your reasons for wanting to enter the trade. Write out your "game plan" for how you intend to manage the trade once a buy signal is triggered, and devise a strategy to cope with any unforeseen circumstances that may arise out of leftfield.

Once you have thoroughly documented your methodology for the trade and it is time to execute the trade, place the required stops using your money management rules and then calmly and patiently sit back, relax and have confidence in your trading plan. You must then develop the discipline to let the trade run its course, knowing that you have done everything humanly possible to achieve a profitable outcome for that trade.

Remember, it does not matter how good your trading plan is—if you do not have the commitment and discipline to follow the plan, you will not succeed long term.

Conclusion

Achieving Financial Independence

"The road to success is always under construction."

Arnold Palmer

Now that you understand the golden rules and trading tools you need to implement to become successful in the stock market, will you take the bull by the horns and create your blissful reality or will you be one of those people who never quite finds the time to do what they know they should? I say "blissful" because that's what so many strive to achieve, yet, so few reach their target.

What are your dreams and desires, not just when it comes to trading, but in life?

Many of you will have read or watched Alice in Wonderland by Lewis Carroll as a child. One of the greatest exchanges is the dialogue between Alice and the Cat:

"Would you tell me, please, which way I ought to go from here?" says Alice

"That depends a good deal on where you want to get to," says the Cat

"I don't much care where," says Alice

"Then it doesn't matter which way you go," says the Cat

Do you know where you are headed? What traits and behaviours will you display on your journey?

Without an end, there is no start. Without a why (your blissful reality), you will be like Alice, who does not care where she ends up. What does your finish line look like?

Success does not come by accident; it is created

Your attitude towards money will play a major role in determining how confident you are when it comes to handling your investments and, in turn, how much wealth you will create in your life. Indeed, many of the issues that hold us back in life and act as barriers to achieving our goals, particularly our financial goals, are the beliefs we inherited from our parents and the surrounding environment during our upbringing.

Many of you will be familiar with the statement: "Your attitude determines your altitude in life." This holds true for every aspect of our lives. Simply put, if you change your attitude, you will change your life. How many of you focus your attention on what you don't have? Unfortunately, what you focus your attention on becomes more real.

Being successful is not gained solely through increasing your knowledge—it is gained by applying it in combination with an increased understanding of yourself.

So, how do you change your attitude? You need to focus your attention on what you want to achieve and then take action. Being successful is not gained solely through increasing your knowledge—it is gained by applying it in combination with an increased understanding of yourself.

How many of you have observed people whom you consider to be successful— have you ever noticed that they all seem to possess similar characteristics? The majority I have observed have a drive and passion for life, which seems to be linked to a strong purpose in mind. They usually have a strategy or a plan of attack as to how they are going to achieve whatever it is they have set their mind to and they always seem organised.

Unfortunately for some, change invokes a fear of the unknown. And, as author, Suzy Kassem says, "It is this state of fear that kills more dreams than failure ever will." While fear is a reaction, courage is a decision; changing your attitude and taking action to achieve your goals will support you as you work towards your blissful reality.

There is no particular science or magic about the characteristics of successful people—it is all within our reach if we have the discipline to implement a few simple steps. Although simple, the steps that follow are profound if you choose to work with them; they will help you make significant changes in your life, particularly when it comes to achieving financial independence.

Know what you want

The first step to success is to know what you want—what you want to have, what you want to be and what you want to achieve. This may be hard to identify if you have not previously given this much thought—but it is essential to your success in every aspect of your life. The best way to determine what you want is to make a list of your dreams and desires. In preparing this list, you need to ask yourself these four profound questions:

- Why?
- Why not?
- Why not me?
- Why not now?

Often, the way forward may seem as clear as mud, that is, until you write it down. From this list, select the dreams and desires that ignite the most passion and drive in you; these are the areas that you will likely commit to following through with initially—as they become the goals you focus your attention on.

For example, if your goal is to become consistently profitable in the stock market then you need to **trade with a purpose in mind**. In other words, you need to know and understand why you are trading, as this will assist you to apply appropriate strategies to ensure you get the results you are seeking. Remember, if you do not know where you are going, how do you know when you will get there? The more specific you are in your purpose, the better your trading plan will be and the less stress you will experience with your trading.

Take action

You now need to make a commitment to take action. That is, the action that will bring about the achievement of your goals. This may seem obvious, but the main characteristic of high achievers is that they actually take action to make something happen rather than just talking or dreaming about it.

Taking action means being personally accountable for your current situation and deciding to rise above it by demonstrating the ownership necessary for you to achieve the results you desire. Accountability is something you need to display every day, not just when it suits you.

A good friend and mentor of mine once told me to surround myself with people who expect more from me than I do of myself. He referred to them as "unreasonable friends". These are the people who help keep you accountable; they don't accept excuses when it comes to your journey to achieving your goals.

In the stock market, accountability means taking responsibility for how you approach your trading so that you achieve the outcomes you desire. This means **taking a disciplined approach to trading**. In other words, you need to develop a clear trading strategy and stick to your trading plan. Remember, success does not come by accident; it is created.

You have probably heard people refer to those who are successful as lucky. However, when you speak to the person who's been labelled lucky, you often find that it is their consistent application and discipline that creates their success, not luck. Successful people do not wait for luck to come their way; they make it happen. The right action coupled with the right knowledge will result in prosperity.

Observe the results of what you do

You need to be able to observe and document the things that happen as a result of your behaviour—in other words, you need to identify whether your actions are bringing you closer to your goal or hindering you. Our behaviour is generally a reflection of the beliefs we hold. So documenting what may be helping or hindering you can help you identify certain beliefs or patterns that may impede you on your journey to achieving your desired outcome.

I have read literally dozens of books on success, from biographies to studies on how to create wealth and how people achieved their success. The overwhelming message that came from each of these books is that successful people make more mistakes than anyone else. But the one key factor that pushes them to achieve their goals, on a consistent basis, is their attitude towards and how they handle their mistakes.

Rather than give up or move on, they take the time to learn from their mistakes, which consequently strengthens their conviction that achieving their goals is within their grasp. So, when faced with a challenge that is hindering you, take responsibility for it and take the time to learn from it. Keep your attention focused on the end goal.

In the stock market, this means **developing a positive attitude to trading**, as your attitude will definitely affect your outcome. Remember, trading is one of the few things you can do where you know from the outset you will lose money. This may result from being over-confident and failing to follow your trading plan, or because you have become too emotionally entangled in a trade; either way, you need to own it, learn from it and move on. It is inevitable that, as you grow and develop your skills, you will make mistakes. It is your attitude towards these mistakes that will determine your long-term success.

Know what motivates you, understand your limitations and become familiar with your strengths. The reality is that trading is 20 per cent technical knowledge and 80 per cent attitude (which dictates how you approach your trading).

Be prepared to change your behaviour until you get the results you want

There are many reasons why we tend to resist change, but one of the most common is ego. This powerful, yet unproductive, trait tends to get in the way of our success, as it acts like a blindfold, keeping us from opening our mind to other possibilities. Another common reason we resist change is pride. Pride and a strong ego can become quite a lethal combination, particularly in the stock market.

How many of you have spent money on something you've found hasn't gotten you the result you want? Yet, you felt justified continuing down the same path because you didn't want to believe you wasted your money. This is very common in the stock market; individuals invest thousands attending courses or buying software in an effort to find the "holy grail" and, as a result, prefer to hang onto ineffective trading strategies in an attempt to create a preferred outcome.

No doubt most of you will have heard the definition of "insanity"—doing the same thing over and over and expecting a different result. If you find the outcome you want doesn't manifest itself as quickly as you would like, step back and put on your creative thinking hat. While you cannot change the past, you can change the future. Given this, it pays to look at the other options you have that will help you get what you want. Once you identify them, you then need to take action.

I have never met a consistently profitable trader who has told me that they got there through sheer luck. I know the more I have applied myself, the luckier I have become. All of those who have achieved success followed four simple steps, as follows:

- They set goals and reviewed them periodically—they focused on what they wanted to achieve.

- They acquired relevant knowledge and developed their skills—they took action.

- They refined what they learnt—they observed the results of what they did.

- They developed a healthy trading psychology—they changed their behaviour to get results.

Given the simplicity of these four steps, some of you may be tempted to bypass them and find something more complex or demanding. Let me assure you, however, that if you follow through and implement them, you will be well rewarded—indeed, your investment will be repaid many times over.

Time is the currency of success

Time is money—it's a phrase we have all heard countless times, but what does it really mean? Once you learn to place value on each and every hour in the day, you'll discover a new level of productivity that will unlock growth like you have never experienced before.

Time is a currency. You can choose what you want to spend it on in the same way that you choose how you spend your pay cheque. When we consider time as a currency, we all sit on a level playing field. Every single one of us lives a twenty-four hour day. Most of us work for eight hours and sleep for eight hours. That leaves us with eight hours to play. What can you achieve if you invest this time deliberately?

Make the most of your day by investing in some "me time" to rejuvenate yourself. According to research, the five most effective ways of managing stress are: watching TV or movies; spending time with family and friends; focusing on the positives; listening to music; and reading. With 80 per cent effectiveness, there's no harm in setting aside a few hours each night to unwind and reset for the day ahead.

So the question remains: Are you willing to spend the remainder of your time deliberately and intelligently so that you move closer to achieving your financial goals?

How will you account for your time in order to achieve the success you desire? Your boss values your time by paying you an hourly rate, so it is important that you place a monetary value on the time you dedicate to becoming financially independent. Knowledge is power; pipedreams will remain just that without effort and accountability.

So, ask yourself: How much is your time worth? We all have the same bank balance: twenty-four hours. How will you invest your time?

The journey

I assume, since you are still reading this book, that you are ready to take advantage of the knowledge you have gained and the rewards that trading the stock market can provide. Your challenge now, having discovered the information in this book, is to work out what you need to do in order to achieve the financial goals you desire. Reading this book is not enough. To reap the financial rewards, you need to put what you have read into practice. When you put down this book, you can go on as you always have or you can make a concerted effort to change your destiny.

If you are serious about becoming consistently profitable in the long term, I encourage you to re-read this book until you completely understand how you can put these tools and strategies into practice. You may want to begin by paper trading a portfolio (test the theories by trading hypothetically) to build up your confidence. In fact, I recommend you do this to prove to yourself that the strategies in this book can work for you. Do not blindly follow what I or anyone else says unless you are willing to test it for yourself. Once you are comfortable and achieving good returns, you can take the leap of faith and invest your money in the stock market with confidence.

Alternatively, you may want to consider dipping your toe in the stock market and investing in only one company at a time. Whichever way you decide to get started, I know from the experience of working with many others just like you that you will enjoy the rewards that will come from building and managing a profitable portfolio.

"In the end, we only regret the chances we didn't take..."
Lewis Carroll

I wish you well on your journey and hope that what you've learned in this book will set you on the path to financial independence.

About the Author

Dale Gillham is "one of Australia's most respected analysts" (Wealth Creator Magazine, Nov/Dec 2004). A sought-after key note speaker and author of the bestselling book *How to Beat the Managed Funds by 20%*, he has assisted thousands of traders and investors around Australia and throughout the world to become confident and profitable, not only in the stock market but also in other investment vehicles.

Tired of an industry saturated with fancy marketing and quick-fix gimmicks, Dale co-founded Wealth Within to provide genuine education as well as independent investment advice to traders and investors who have become disillusioned with the industry for one reason or another.

Dale has over 25 years' experience in various sectors of the investment industry, including banking, financial planning, stock market education and professional trading. For more than twenty years, Dale has achieved profitable returns in his private trading while sharing his knowledge and guidance with others to help them reach their goals when it comes to financial independence.

An excellent and expert motivator, teacher and investment manager, Dale is in his element when helping others achieve their financial goals.

Glossary

All Ordinaries Index (All Ords): This measures the level of stock prices at any given time for a sample of major companies listed on the ASX in order to determine the overall performance of the stock market.

Bear market: When stock prices are falling sharply.

Blue chip: Shares in a company that are highly valued. These types of companies are known for their ability to generate solid profits in the good times and hold up in the bad. An example of a blue chip stock would be one of the four major banks.

Brokerage: The fee paid to a stockbroking firm for buying or selling stocks.

Bull market: When stock prices are generally rising.

Buy and hold: An investing strategy based on the historical tendency of the market to rise over time.

Capital: The initial funds invested.

Capital gains: Additions to investing capital due to a rise in the stock price.

Capital gains tax: Tax on a profit from the sale of capital assets such as stocks.

Compounding: The ability of an asset to generate earnings that are then reinvested to generate further earnings, for example, "interest earned on interest".

Contracts for Difference (CFDs): A leveraged instrument which allows a trader to enter into a "contract" to exchange the "difference" between the opening and closing value of the contract, with reference to an underlying instrument.

DAX: The DAX is a stock market exchange that consists of 30 major German blue chip companies that trade on the Frankfurt Stock Exchange.

Diversification: Spreading investments over a variety of investment categories (or sectors within the stock market) to reduce risk.

Dividend: When a company distributes part of its profits back to the shareholders by way of number of cents per share held.

Dividend imputation: Tax credits that are passed on to the shareholder by way of what is called a franked dividend. Imputation credits entitle investors to a tax rebate on tax already paid by an Australian company under the provisions of the Income Tax Assessment Act.

Dividend yield: The dividend shown as a percentage of the last sale price for the stock.

Entry: The price at which you buy a stock.

Exit: The price at which you sell a stock.

Fundamental analysis: A method of evaluating securities by attempting to measure the intrinsic value of a particular stock.

Investment: An asset acquired for the purposes of generating income and capital growth.

Leveraging: The use of borrowed capital to increase the potential return of an investment.

Liquidity: A liquid market is one where you are able to convert assets back to cash quickly as there are enough participants to make buying and selling easy.

Managed fund: A fund that pools investors' money to invest in various asset classes.

Margin call: The requirement for a debt to be reduced if its security loses value.

Margin loan: This allows investors to use their existing stocks to increase their investment portfolio on margin.

Market capitalisation: The total number of shares on issue multiplied by the market price. This can be used to work out the value of the company listed on the exchange.

Market price: The last price that stocks are traded on an exchange or the most recent price or bid offered for the stock.

Offer: The price at which someone is willing to sell the stock.

Paper trade: Hypothetical trading that occurs when investors mimic trades (buys and sells) without actually entering into any monetary transactions.

Peak: To make a peak, you must have a movement up in price followed by a down movement in price.

Portfolio: A term used to describe a group of assets held by an investor as a whole.

Price earnings ratio: This shows the number of times the price covers the earnings per share.

Securities: A general term used for all stocks, debentures, notes, bills, government and semi-government bonds, and so on.

Stop loss: An order placed with a broker to sell at a specified price after a given stop price has been reached or passed.

Technical analysis: A method of evaluating securities by analysing patterns generated by market activity, such as past prices and volume.

Trading on margin: Refer to leveraging

Trend: The general direction of the price of an asset or market in general.

Trend analysis: A type of technical analysis used to determine or locate significant trends in a stock.

Trough: To make a trough, you need to have a down movement in price followed by an upward movement in price.

Volatility: In general, volatility is a measure of the tendency of a security to rise or fall sharply within a short period of time.

Endnotes

1. Hoyle, S., 6 December 2003, "The argument for putting all your eggs in one basket", *The Age,*

2. Conlin, A. and Miettunen, J., 15 August 2017, "Personality Traits and Portfolio Tilts Towards Value and Size", *https://papers.ssrn.com/sol3/papers.cfm?abstract_id=3018383*

3. Rodriguez, D and Shea, T., 8 December 2011, "What is the Number One Mistake Forex Traders Make?", *https://www.dailyfx.com/forex/education/trading_tips/daily_trading_lesson/2011/12/08/What_is_the_Number_One_Mistake_Forex_Traders_Make.html*

4. Owen, A., 21 November 2014, "Who Wins? Australia versus US in local Shares" *https://cuffelinks.com.au/wins-australian-versus-us-investors-local-shares/*

5. "Types of managed funds and how they perform long term", *https://www.canstar.com.au/managed-funds/types-of-managed-funds-and-how-they-perform-long-term/*

6. 2014 American Trader Study, *Scottrade Inc.*

Index

Wealth Within

Wealth Within is focused on helping individuals maximise their investments in the stock market. The company was co-founded by Dale Gillham in 2002 to provide a range of services to traders and investors who understand the need to invest in the stock market to achieve their financial goals.

The highest standard in education...

With so much hype surrounding the share market, Wealth Within has sought to raise the bar in the industry by setting quality standards in the level of education being delivered by developing Australia's first and only Diploma of Share Trading and Investment.

This means we guarantee you the highest quality share trading education available today. It also means that our courses are independent evidence that you will be competent in the techniques and strategies taught.

As a way of introducing you to the quality of our education, we also provide an introductory course known as Trading Mentor.

Let us invest for you...

By listening to our clients, we understand that for some, your time is limited and you may not want to watch over your own portfolio. This is why we offer our Individually Managed Account service that delivers returns which outperform the market over the medium to long term. Using proven and disciplined investment techniques, our aim is to support our clients maximise the returns on their investments.

For more information, visit www.wealthwithin.com.au or phone 1300 858 272 or Melbourne direct on 9290 9999.

Where can you learn more about Dale Gillham and Wealth Within

To stay up to date with what is happening in the market, **join us on Wealth Within**: https://www.youtube.com/results?search_query=Wealth+Within

You can also watch Dale on his Flixx cable network show, **Talking Wealth** by visiting https://www.talkingwealth.com

Thank you for reading this book. If you would like to make a suggestion for future books, please email info@wealthwithin.com.au